ROBERT SCHUMANN: PIANO CONCERTO

Offering a concise introduction to one of the most important and influential piano concertos in the history of Western music, this handbook provides an example of the productive interaction of music history, music theory and music analysis. It combines an account of the work's genesis, Schumann's earlier, unsuccessful attempts to compose in the genre and the evolving conception of the piano concerto evident in his critical writing with a detailed yet accessible analysis of each movement, which draws on the latest research into the theory and analysis of nineteenth-century instrumental forms. This handbook also reconstructs the Concerto's critical reception, its performance history in centres such as London, Vienna, Leipzig and New York and its discography, before surveying piano concertos composed under its influence in the century after its completion, including well-known concertos by Brahms, Grieg, Tchaikovsky and Rachmaninov, as well as lesser-known music by Scharwenka, Rubinstein, Beach, MacDowell and Stanford.

JULIAN HORTON is Professor of Music at Durham University. A past president of the Society for Music Analysis, he is the author of *Bruckner's Symphonies: Analysis, Reception and Cultural Politics* (2004) and *Brahms' Piano Concerto No. 2, Op. 83: Analytical and Contextual Studies* (2017) and editor of *The Cambridge Companion to the Symphony* (2013).

NEW CAMBRIDGE MUSIC HANDBOOKS

Series Editor

NICOLE GRIMES, UNIVERSITY OF CALIFORNIA, IRVINE

The New Cambridge Music Handbooks series provides accessible introductions to landmarks in music history, written by leading experts in their field. Encompassing a wide range of musical styles and genres, it embraces the music of hitherto under-represented creators as well as re-imagining works from the established canon. It will enrich the musical experience of students, scholars, listeners and performers alike.

Books in the Series

Hensel: String Quartet in E flat
Benedict Taylor

Berlioz: Symphonie Fantastique
Julian Rushton

Margaret Bonds: The Montgomery Variations and Du Bois 'Credo'
John Michael Cooper

Robert Schumann: Piano Concerto
Julian Horton

Schoenberg: 'Night Music', Verklärte Nacht and Erwartung
Arnold Whittall

Forthcoming Titles

Schubert: The 'Great' Symphony in C major
Suzannah Clark

Bach: The Cello Suites
Edward Klorman

Clara Schumann: Piano Concerto in A minor Op. 7
Julie Pedneault-Deslauriers

Donizetti: Lucia di Lammermoor
Mark Pottinger

Beethoven: String Quartet Op. 130
Elaine Sisman

Louise Farrenc: Nonet for Winds and Strings
Marie Sumner Lott

Cavalleria rusticana and Pagliacci
Alexandra Wilson

ROBERT SCHUMANN: PIANO CONCERTO

JULIAN HORTON
Durham University

CAMBRIDGE
UNIVERSITY PRESS

Shaftesbury Road, Cambridge CB2 8EA, United Kingdom

One Liberty Plaza, 20th Floor, New York, NY 10006, USA

477 Williamstown Road, Port Melbourne, VIC 3207, Australia

314–321, 3rd Floor, Plot 3, Splendor Forum, Jasola District Centre, New Delhi – 110025, India

103 Penang Road, #05–06/07, Visioncrest Commercial, Singapore 238467

Cambridge University Press is part of Cambridge University Press & Assessment, a department of the University of Cambridge.

We share the University's mission to contribute to society through the pursuit of education, learning and research at the highest international levels of excellence.

www.cambridge.org
Information on this title: www.cambridge.org/9781316512586

DOI: 10.1017/9781009067843

First published 2024

A catalogue record for this publication is available from the British Library.

A Cataloging-in-Publication data record for this book is available from the Library of Congress

ISBN 978-1-316-51258-6 Hardback
ISBN 978-1-009-06829-1 Paperback

To Sean

for all the wonderful conversations

CONTENTS

FIGURES

TABLES

MUSIC EXAMPLES

List of Music Examples

ACKNOWLEDGEMENTS

The completion of this book has been made possible by the generosity of some remarkable people. I would like to acknowledge the kind assistance of the Heinrich Heine Institut, Düsseldorf, and especially Christian Liedtke, for making the manuscript of Schumann's Piano Concerto available. Gratitude is also due to Eleanor Roberts, archivist of the Hallé Orchestra Concert Society, for providing a complete performance history of Op. 54 in the Hallé's programmes up to 1900. Research into the Romantic piano concerto that is foundational to the broader historical view adopted in this book was facilitated by an Irish Research Council Fellowship; ongoing collaborations with Steven Vande Moortele, Benedict Taylor, Peter H. Smith and Paul Wingfield have also vitally informed its content and arguments. The text has benefitted from one anonymous reader's careful scrutiny, whose many constructive observations were most welcome. Sean Eddie offered invaluable help on matters of Saxon history, a field to which I am a newcomer, and on German history in general; and fascinating conversations about Op. 54 with the pianists Tim Horton and Paul Lewis have inflected the book's content and enhanced my appreciation of this wonderful piece. I am, as ever, deeply appreciative of Kate Brett's guidance and support; the production team at Cambridge University Press have also been customarily outstanding: Sally Evans-Darby, Nigel Graves, Preethika Ramalingam and Abi Sears. Table 2.1 is reproduced from Claudia Macdonald, *Robert Schumann and the Piano Concerto* (New York: Routledge 2005), 56, by kind permission of Routledge. Figures 2.1 and 2.2 reproduce pages from the manuscript of Schumann's Piano Concerto, by kind permission of the Heinrich Heine Institut, Düsseldorf.

Acknowledgements

I reserve special thanks to Nicole Grimes for encouraging me to write this book, for her limitless kindness at every stage of its genesis, writing and production, for her stalwart assistance during my Irish Research Council Fellowship and for her wise counsel on so many matters in the analysis and interpretation of nineteenth-century music, and much else besides. Finally, profound gratitude is due, as always, to my family – Janet, Emma and Toby – for their love and support.

INTRODUCTION
Situating Schumann's Piano Concerto

'A Worthy Monument to the Sanity of Art': Patterns of Reception

One day during a school music lesson, my teacher turned to me and stated, somewhat provocatively, that 'everything Schumann wrote after 1840 was poor, except for the Piano Concerto'. As I have since discovered, he was not expressing an original opinion. The idea that Schumann achieved much in the piano music of the 1830s and the songs of 1840 but faded into mediocrity as soon as he tried to compose large-scale orchestral works has been a regular theme of Schumann reception for more than one hundred years, and is at least as old as Felix Weingartner's pronouncement, dating from 1897, that Schumann's symphonies were 'in no wise among his most important works'. Whereas 'In [Schumann's] pianoforte pieces the invention of little, but very expressive, themes ... is very characteristic', for Weingartner 'in his great symphonies he does not succeed with these themes and themelets, however warm and beautiful the feeling may have been from which they sprang.'[1]

The view that the Piano Concerto, Op. 54 is an exception to this rule is also often expressed. Composed between 1841 and 1845, it has secured perennial membership of the performing canon, remaining a favourite of pianists and audiences alike; and its critical reception does not evidence suspicion or hostility to anything like the extent encountered by Schumann's other large-scale works of the 1840s and 1850s. Whereas the symphonies have endured despite their critical reception, and the oratorio *Das Paradies und die Peri*, the opera *Genoveva* and the monumental *Szenen aus Goethes Faust* have drifted to the margins of musical history, Op. 54 belongs to a select group of piano concerti which continues to define the genre's post-classical evolution in the public and scholarly imagination.

The Piano Concerto has remained comparatively immune to other tendencies in Schumann reception. The habit of hitching the meaning and value of Schumann's music to biographical factors has largely bypassed Op. 54. The piano works composed between 1835 and 1840 are invariably regarded as the products of unrequited love, fuelled by the prohibition placed, by her father Friedrich, on Schumann's relationship with Clara Wieck, which blossomed in 1835 but was only consummated in marriage in September 1840, following a bitter and protracted legal dispute.[2] Schumann himself acknowledged the link, explaining in a letter to Heinrich Dorn of 5 September 1839 that 'much in my music embodies, and indeed can only be understood against the background of the battles that Clara cost me'.[3] Yet although Op. 54's first movement, completed as a standalone *Phantasie* in 1841, owed its genesis to an engagement with the genre that stretched back more than a decade and intersected in multiple ways with Robert's developing relationship with Clara, commentators on Op. 54 have generally not sought interpretations akin to John Daverio's intensely biographical readings of the compositions from the Piano Sonata, Op. 11 to the *Nachtstücke*, Op. 23, which he describes collectively as 'musical love letters'.[4]

The works after 1840 – including the four symphonies, the major chamber music, *Das Paradies und die Peri*, *Genoveva* and the *Szenen aus Goethes Faust* – are more often perceived through a medical lens, reflecting Schumann's struggle against mental and physical illness, which arguably had its origins in the possible symptoms of primary syphilis he reported in 1831, and which culminated in his attempted suicide in Düsseldorf in February 1854 and subsequent committal to the sanatorium at Endenich, where he died in July 1856. Metaphors of incapacity abound in the literature, often highlighting an apparent inability to think in the large-scale, developmental ways necessary for the composition of symphonic forms, a general incompetence in the handling of orchestration, which, we are told, worsened as his illness advanced, and an inept feeling for musical drama, which accounts for *Genoveva*'s lasting obscurity. Carl Dahlhaus' views on the Symphony No. 1, Op. 38 are broadly representative:

Schumann's main motive [in the first movement] ... permeates virtually the entire movement . . .. It is clear that both the lyric tone of Schumann's idea, which is more suitable to a character piece than to a symphony, and his lack of melodic variety work against the large-scale form he was seeking to create . . .. However shrewdly Schumann calculated the form of this movement, by substituting the motivic unity of the character piece for that of the Beethoven symphony he became embroiled in contradictions between lyricism and monumentality ... that led not so much to a productive dialectic as to a mutual paralysis of its various components.[5]

For Dahlhaus, as for others, Schumann was a miniaturist who could not translate the idiom of his piano and song cycles into symphonic forms. The resulting 'paralysis', which Dahlhaus describes in suggestively medical language, amounts to a kind of compositional infirmity that incapacitates musical form.[6]

The Symphony No. 2, Op. 61 has proved especially prone to this kind of diagnosis. Composed in 1845 in the midst of the health crisis that began during the Russian tour undertaken with Clara in 1844 and persisted into 1846, Op. 61 is often heard as symbolic of Schumann's battle with mental and physical illness, again responding to his scattered comments on the work. Mosco Carner's version of the argument is extreme, but not atypical. Carner, like Dahlhaus, considered Schumann 'a lyric miniaturist' whose 'self-chosen domain was first the short self-contained piano piece and song' and who was consequently 'unable to invent true symphonic themes'.[7] Schumann confronted the challenge of an overarching Beethovenian narrative directly in Op. 61 by seeking to give symphonic expression to 'a terrifying personal experience' in which 'the spectre of madness was before him'.[8] Carner goes beyond Dahlhaus by regarding Schumann's infirmity as explicitly gendered: Op. 61 fails because Schumann's depressive psychology evidences an inherent femininity, which ill equipped him to express personal struggle in symphonic form: 'Schumann was no heroic figure: emotionally a feminine type [!], he must have found the subject of which he wished to treat ... fundamentally uncongenial and beyond his powers. That his mental state at the time was an important factor in contributing to the pathetic failure of this work, is not to be gainsaid.'[9]

Opp. 54 and 61 are contemporaneous works – the final date entered on Op. 54's autograph score is 29 July 1845; the Symphony was begun in December of that year – but critical opinion seldom saddles the Piano Concerto with comparable psychiatric baggage.[10] When Donald Francis Tovey described it as 'a worthy monument to the sanity of art' which 'illuminates the tragic pathos of Schumann's later years' but 'is itself untouched', he captured the persisting sense that the Concerto somehow stands apart from the medical tribulations afflicting other large-scale compositions of this period.[11] This feeling is echoed by Dahlhaus, who registered no problems of generic inconsistency or structural paralysis in Op. 54 akin to those he detected in the 'Spring' Symphony because for him there is no requirement to grasp the Concerto in symphonic terms. Instead, we should construe its first movement as 'a piano piece with orchestral accompaniment, which, despite its unusually large dimensions, is lyrical in tone and monothematic in its form'. Op. 54 is, by this argument, held together by the textural 'unity' that affiliation with the lyric character piece confers. A property that incapacitates the 'Spring' Symphony – the use of lyric material in a large-scale orchestral composition – is in this case viewed as formally advantageous. Consequently – and here Op. 54's exceptionalism is patently invoked – Dahlhaus regarded the work as 'a historically unique, unreduplicatable special instance of the "romantic concerto"'.[12]

Critical approval and popularity notwithstanding, the Piano Concerto has also suffered a degree of neglect in several areas of its reception, reflecting a somewhat scattered response to Schumann's concerti in general. Daverio's characterisation of Schumann's uniquely systematic attitude towards genre is, for example, oddly neglectful of the concerti. Viewing his career panoptically, Daverio was struck by Schumann's successive annexation of genres, going so far as to propose a generic 'system', the formation of which gained momentum in the 1840s, as the major classical categories were broached virtually on a yearly basis. As he explains:

There is no reason to believe that Schumann consciously determined, at a specific point in his career, to exhaust the possibilities of the various musical genres in turn. Yet when we stand back and view his output as a whole, its general outlines emerge with unmistakable clarity: the initial focus on piano music during the

1830s gives way, during the next decade, to song, symphony, chamber music, oratorio, and dramatic music, and finally, in the composer's last years, to a recapitulation of the entire scheme and the addition of church music.[13]

The concerto is conspicuously absent from this list; and yet few genres preoccupied Schumann more consistently across his career or provoked him to seek more radical compositional solutions. In this respect, the publication of Op. 54 by Breitkopf and Härtel in 1846 signalled the fulfilment of an ambition, which had intermittently preoccupied Schumann for nearly twenty years, and which subsequently lingered until the end of his creative life. In addition to Op. 54, he also produced concerti for cello (Op. 129 of 1850) and violin (completed in 1853 and published posthumously), as well as works that are manifestly concerti by any other name (the *Concertstück* for four horns and orchestra, Op. 86 of 1849) and single-movement compositions in dialogue with concerto principles (the Introduction and Allegro Appassionato, Op. 92 of 1849; the Introduction and Concert-Allegro, Op. 134 of 1853, both for piano and orchestra). Stalled attempts at concerto composition are a recurrent feature of his output before 1841; and as a critic, Schumann maintained a lively conversation with the piano concerti of his time, an encounter that stimulated him to commit his ideas to paper as both composer and journalist. Although his engagement with the concerto is perhaps less orderly than his progress in song, symphony, chamber music and oratorio between 1840 and 1845, it nevertheless forms a circumscribing thread in these years, which is not easily accommodated in Daverio's 'system'.[14]

In addition to Op. 54's significance for Schumann's career, the work is also pivotal to the piano concerto's history. The debates with which Schumann engaged in the 1830s – ranging across questions of form, style, genre, virtuosity, organology, aesthetics and cultural politics – and the substantive alternatives he explored in Op. 54 capture critical issues in the genre's post-classical development;[15] Op. 54 moreover served as a clear compositional model for many later-century examples. Yet our grasp of the work's place in musical history remains somewhat uncertain.

Pace Dahlhaus, historians seeking to classify Schumann's Piano Concerto have tended to regard it as a seminal contribution to the 'symphonic' concerto, a version of the genre that emerged in the mid-nineteenth century in response to the superficiality and excess of early-century virtuoso concerti. The symphonic concerto is, however, a rather unstable category, which adequately accounts neither for Op. 54 nor for its relationship with other allegedly 'symphonic' works. Often, the compositions housed within it have little in common except for an apparent suspicion of early-century virtuosity. Schumann, to be sure, was highly critical of the virtuoso aesthetic, especially as practised by Parisian composers. But his engagement with virtuoso concerti is complex; and our modern understanding of this umbrella term is frequently inconsistent with Schumann's grasp of the repertoire. As Juan Martin Koch rightly observes, in seeking to comprehend the genre's mid-nineteenth-century evolution, 'it would be a mistake to focus one-sidedly on those aesthetic principles which, from about 1840 onwards, gained increasing importance with the help of the dichotomy "virtuoso" versus "symphonic"'.[16] Concerti ordinarily classified, and just as often ridiculed, for their association with virtuosity are themselves something of an analytical and theoretical *terra incognita*, knowledge of which profoundly alters our understanding both of what Schumann was hoping to achieve and of what our theoretical tools for the analysis of piano concerti should consist, if we have any aspiration towards historical accuracy. Looking towards the late nineteenth and early twentieth centuries, few concerti left their mark so obviously on the repertoire, especially in the Russian and Scandinavian contexts. It is not hyperbolic to argue that Op. 54 functions as a kind of generic fulcrum which synthesises compositional problems accruing from the early nineteenth century and defines a subsequent field of practice stretching as far as the First World War. But this critical and compositional legacy has been left comparatively untouched; the obvious influence Op. 54 exerted on concerti by Grieg, Tchaikovsky, Rachmaninov and many others remains to be explored in any detail.

Analytical commentaries on Op. 54 are also comparatively scarce and have focused predominantly on the first movement, thanks perhaps to its original conception as a single-movement *Phantasie* and close engagement with the problems that Schumann diagnosed in his critical writings of the 1830s. Commentators have called attention to the *Phantasie*'s nascent 'two-dimensionality' – its tactic of embedding aspects of a three-movement concerto cycle within a one-movement sonata form – as well as its high degree of material integration and tendency to favour thematic processes over overt displays of pianism or rhetorical excess.[17] Fascinating issues of syntax in this movement, and the questions it poses for modern formal theory, however, await thorough scrutiny; and the second and third movements, which Schumann added in 1845, have received notably scant attention, an oversight that is especially unfortunate in view of their complex relationship with the first movement and the Finale's formal, rhythmic and metrical riches.[18]

Finally, Schumann's Concerto raises unaddressed socio-political questions. Concerti engender and reflect social relations in a unique way because a discourse between the individual and the collective is built into their generic identity. The strategic management of solo-orchestral interactions is central to this issue and has constituted both a major preoccupation of composers across the concerto's history and an important barometer of their changing social environment. When Schumann diagnosed what he regarded as the flaws in many of the concerti composed in the early decades of the nineteenth century, he pointed to problems that were social and political as much as aesthetic, having to do with the mediation of individual autonomy and collective responsibility in a post-Enlightenment society. As we will see, political idealism and questions of national identity often lurked close to the surface in these debates. To analyse the ways in which Op. 54 reconceives the genre's forms and material processes is therefore necessarily to tackle the question of its social responsibilities and political aspirations. The interaction of 'symphonic' features with residues of the virtuoso style and the lyric elements identified by Dahlhaus feeds directly into the Concerto's dialogue with cultural politics, helping to shape a vision of the genre as an allegory of the aesthetic state.

Objectives

It is this book's principal aim to address these various issues by offering a complete analytical conspectus of Schumann's Piano Concerto, framed by an account of its genesis and of its critical and compositional reception. Any deep engagement with Op. 54 needs additionally to deal with the complex questions of form and generic identity that attend the nineteenth-century piano concerto more generally. In the field of music theory especially, conceptions of concerto form have been heavily dependent on canonical repertoire, and above all on ideas centred on the reception of Mozart. Schumann, however, was vitally engaged with a body of early-nineteenth-century works which has little presence in the performing canon or the literature on concerto form, but which is an essential component of Op. 54's pre-history. Before engaging in detail with the work itself, I consequently appraise important trends in the theory of concerto form in Chapter 1 and bring them into dialogue with the genre's post-classical history, as the compositional milieu in which Schumann's ideas about piano concerti germinated, before sketching Op. 54's genesis and the evolution of his approach to the genre in Chapter 2. Chapters 3 and 4 then develop an analytical reading of the Concerto, drawing on the framework established in Chapters 1 and 2. For the benefit of readers unfamiliar with the jargon of modern formal theory, I supplement the analyses in these chapters with Appendix I, which lists and defines my terminology. Chapter 5 appraises aspects of the work's performance history and critical reception and also examines concerti of the later nineteenth and early twentieth centuries, which betray traces of Op. 54's formal, stylistic, material and aesthetic fingerprints. Chapter 5's conspectus of performance history is supported by Appendix II, which compiles a representative discography.

My school music teacher was, I think, quite wrong about Schumann's mature instrumental works; to this extent, he was also wrong about Op. 54, which takes its place in the procession of achievements in the 'higher' forms spanning from the Symphony No. 1 of 1841 to the Symphony No. 3 of 1850 and the *Szenen aus Goethes Faust*, begun in 1844 but not completed until 1853. Reappraising the rich array of theoretical, analytical, historical and cultural-political issues that intersect in Op. 54 consequently affords fresh grounds for rethinking Schumann's contributions across the major classical genres.

Notes

1. Felix Weingartner, *Die Symphonie nach Beethoven* (Leipzig: Breitkopf und Härtel, 1897) and *The Symphony Since Beethoven*, translated by M. B. Dutton (Boston, MA: Oliver Ditson, 1904), excerpted as 'Schumann as Symphonist (1904–1906)', in R. Larry Todd, ed., *Schumann and His World* (Princeton, NJ: Princeton University Press, 1994), 375–84, at 377 and 378. Weingartner was also highly critical of Schumann's orchestration, adumbrating a view that is repeated in English-language literature across the twentieth century. Compare Weingartner's views with those of Adolph Schubring, published in 1861, who holds that Schumann 'is at his greatest in his epic works', which for Schubring includes the dramatic works (*Das Paradies und die Peri, Manfred, Genoveva* and *Faust*), the symphonies ('orchestral novels') and string quartets, and the early piano cycles, without differentiation. See 'Schumanniana No. 4: The Present Musical Epoch and Robert Schumann's Position in Music History (1861)', translated by John Michael Cooper in Todd, ed., *Schumann and His World*, 362–74, at 371.
2. For an account of Robert and Clara's legal dispute with Friedrich Wieck, see John Daverio, *Robert Schumann: Herald of a New Poetic Age* (Oxford: Oxford University Press, 1997), 182–96.
3. Quoted in Daverio, *Robert Schumann*, 131.
4. Ibid., 131–81 and especially 132, where Daverio notes that 'In Schumann's compositions art and life continually engage in a kind of chemical process of transformation. "Biographical" subjects, ranging from place names to human beings, are converted into "aesthetic" subjects, musical materials, and then back again into more tangible poetic designations.' One exception to Op. 54's exemption from readings of this kind can be found in Joseph Kerman, 'The Concertos', in Beate Perrey, ed., *The Cambridge Companion to Schumann* (Cambridge: Cambridge University Press, 2007), 173–94, at 178, where Kerman briefly suggests that the head motive of the first movement's main theme – C–B–A – alludes to Clara.
5. Carl Dahlhaus, *Nineteenth-Century Music*, translated by J. Bradford Robinson (Berkeley: University of California Press, 1989), 159–60. It is worth noting that Dahlhaus' original German is subtly different to Robinson's translation, which renders 'der Mangel an melodischer Variabilität' as 'his lack of material variability' rather than 'its [i.e. the material's] lack of variability', implying a fault in Schumann's technique which Dahlhaus attributes to the material itself. I am grateful to Steven Vande Moortele for pointing this out.
6. Dahlhaus' phrase here is 'sich gegenseitig lähmten': literally, lyricism and monumentality 'paralyse each other'.

7. Mosco Carner, 'The Orchestral Music', in Gerald Abraham, ed., *Schumann: A Symposium* (London: Oxford University Press, 1952), 176–244, at 177.
8. Ibid., 180–1.
9. Ibid., 220–1.
10. On the Symphony's genesis, see Daverio, *Robert Schumann*, 315–16.
11. Tovey, 'CXXI: Schumann, Pianoforte Concerto in A Minor, Op. 54', *Essays in Musical Analysis*, vol. III *Vol. 3, Concertos* (London: Oxford University Press, 1936), 182–4, at 182.
12. Dahlhaus, *Nineteenth-Century Music*, 141.
13. Daverio, *Robert Schumann*, 218–19.
14. A conspectus of Schumann's concerti is offered in Kerman, 'The Concertos', in Perrey, ed., *The Cambridge Companion to Schumann*.
15. This context has been most substantially and systematically explored by Claudia Macdonald; see *Robert Schumann and the Piano Concerto* (New York: Routledge, 2005).
16. Juan Martin Koch, *Das Klavierkonzert des 19. Jahrhunderts und der Kategorie des Symphonischen* (Sinzing: Studio, 2001), 42: 'Zudem währe es verfehlt, den Blick einseitig auf diejenigen ästhetischen Prinzipen zu lenken, die seit etwa 1840 unter Zuhilfenahme der sich nun zum Topos verfestigenden Dichotomie "virtuos" versus "symphonisch" immer stärker an Bedeutung gewannen.' Koch defines Schumann's Op. 54 as 'symphonic' because he sees its genesis as part of Schumann's 'road to the symphony' rather than as a work contributing to a separate generic category of 'symphonic' concerti. He writes: 'The effectiveness of the symphonic category can be observed in relation to Robert Schumann's A minor Piano Concerto insofar as this work is often attributed a special significance on his "road to the symphony".' ('Die Wirksamkeit der Kategorie des Symphonischen ist in bezug auf Robert Schumanns a-Moll-Klavierkonzert insofern zu beobachten, als diesem Werk häufig eine besondere Bedeutung auf dessen "Weg zur Symphonie" zugesprochen wird.')
17. The term 'two-dimensionality' is coined by Steven Vande Moortele; see *Two-Dimensional Sonata Form: Form and Cycle in Single-Movement Instrumental Works by Liszt, Strauss, Schoenberg, and Zemlinsky* (Leuven: Leuven University Press, 2009).
18. Koch, for example, allocates ten pages to his analysis of the first movement of Op. 54 and little more than two to the Intermezzo and rondo; see *Das Klavierkonzert des 19. Jahrhunderts und der Kategorie des Symphonischen*, 219–28 and 228–30, respectively. Similarly, Macdonald devotes an entire chapter to the *Phantasie* but little more than eight pages of a much larger chapter to the Intermezzo and Finale; see *Robert Schumann and the Piano Concerto*, 223–46 and 263–71.

RETHINKING THE ROMANTIC PIANO CONCERTO

Contexts and Misconceptions

Attempts to contextualise Schumann's Op. 54 quickly encounter discrepancies, if not open contradictions, between the groundswell of historical information about the Romantic piano concerto and prevailing tendencies in the theoretical and analytical literature. On the one hand, Schumann came to the concerto keenly aware of a diverse, cosmopolitan and widely circulating repertoire, encompassing music by Hummel, Kalkbrenner, Moscheles, Chopin, Field and Herz, among many others, which has often been classified under the rubric of the 'virtuoso' concerto and which collectively defined the genre's stylistic and technical parameters in the first half of the nineteenth century. On the other hand, music theory has relied overwhelmingly on the examples left by Mozart, Beethoven and a very small number of selected successors as the evidential basis for the modelling of concerto forms, an orientation that has strongly inflected perceptions of the nineteenth-century repertoire. To be sure, Schumann's Op. 54 straddles this divide, as a canonical work by a canonical composer. Nevertheless, formal theory's failure to engage with the virtuoso concerto's practices has only impeded the rich analytical understanding of Schumann's contribution.

In general, the narrative advocated by mainstream music theory understands the Romantic piano concerto as part of the reception history of Mozart's concerti. In the English-language literature, at least from Donald Francis Tovey onwards, the idea that Mozart's achievement defines the genre has become a commonplace. Of particular concern for this discourse is the question of how sonata form should be melded with the older ritornello principle, evident in baroque concerti and arias, in what has come to be called concerto first-movement form or, in the terms of James Hepokoski and Warren Darcy's sonata theory, the 'type 5 sonata'.[1] This formal dilemma is unique among instrumental genres. Ritornello forms are recursive and rely on the oscillation between relatively invariant orchestral material and digressive solo episodes, whereas classical sonata form is dramatic and goal-directed, establishing a tonal-thematic dialectic and working towards its resolution. Mozart is usually understood to have perfectly resolved this quandary and subsequent practitioners to have invariably misunderstood his solutions, creating a historical problematic which has informed much subsequent commentary on the genre.

For Tovey, Mozart accessed a kind of generic ideal type, which Tovey called the 'true concerto', central to which is the idea that the opening orchestral ritornello (R1 in the usage of modern formal theory) should resemble a sonata exposition except that the second theme appears in the tonic.[2] Tovey regarded this as essential for two reasons: first, because it leaves the way clear for the soloist to introduce a structural modulation; and second, because a non-tonic orchestral second-theme presentation is the defining event of a symphonic sonata exposition, which means that preserving the modulation for the soloist is vital for differentiating concerti from symphonies.

Tovey indicted most nineteenth-century composers coming to the genre, and prior theorists who attempted to explain it, with failing to understand these essential points because they habitually favoured a double-exposition model of first-movement form, conceived as a platform for virtuosity, in which R1 is at liberty to introduce a modulation for its second theme, which the solo exposition (S1) revisits. Tovey traced this 'error' to Beethoven, specifically his first three piano concerti, Opp. 15, 19 and 37. But Beethoven differs from his contemporaries and successors in that the problem is identified and addressed in his Triple Concerto Op. 56, the R1 of which remains in the tonic, and this solution is refined in the piano concerti Opp. 58 and 73. On the other hand, 'every virtuoso whose imagination is fired with the splendid spectacular effect of a full orchestra as a background for a display of instrumental technique has written concertos that express little else than that effect', the result being 'literally hundreds of works that have not even an academic connexion with the classical idea of concerto form and style'.[3] Beethoven's error was duly replicated, and 'until Brahms came to the rescue [in his Op. 15], the opening tutti of the classical concerto remained a mystery to composers and theorists alike'.[4]

Whereas most Romantic composers walked straight into this trap, Tovey considered both Schumann and Mendelssohn to have avoided it by devising variants of the genre that have no classical precedent at all. Thus Mendelssohn 'may truthfully be said to have destroyed the classical concerto form, inasmuch as his perennially beautiful Violin Concerto and his two somewhat faded pianoforte concertos revealed to all contemporary and later composers an easy way of evading a problem which only Mozart and Beethoven could either state or solve in terms of the highest art'.[5] Similarly, although in Op. 54 Schumann composed 'a very big first move-ment in sonata form, it never professed to be the first movement of a classical concerto'.[6] The solution is the same in both cases: what Hepokoski and Darcy call the 'type 5' first-movement form per-fected by Mozart, which is a hybrid of sonata and ritornello principles, is replaced by a type 3 sonata, which is the 'standard-textbook' sonata consisting of a single exposition, development and recapitulation.

Tovey's perspective suggests a historical narrative, in which the classical type 5 sonata yields, across the nineteenth century, to its type 3 sibling, the result being a progressive narrowing of the generic difference between concerto and symphony. This is the view taken by Hepokoski and Darcy, albeit it without Tovey's critical tilt:

Mozart's concerto-sonata syntheses were continued by Beethoven and others. Eventually, with Mendelssohn especially, the initial ritornello of the Type 5 concerto came to seem redundant, old-fashioned, something that had outworn its original *raison d'être*. With its excision, what had been the favored format for concerto first movements – the Type 5 sonata – collapsed into the Type 3 pattern. At this point the absorption of the concerto into sonata form became complete. The history of the concerto in the eighteenth century and beyond, developing alongside the symphony, is that of gradually being attracted to the latter's principles, finding ways of adapting itself to them while retaining important features of its own identity, but eventually (around the fourth decade of the nineteenth century) succumbing rather totally to them.[7]

This narrative underscores the difference between two nineteenth-century concerto practices which have enjoyed quite different reception histories. Works embracing the type 3 sonata in their first movement are often identified as 'symphonic' concerti, a sub-genre to which Schumann's Op. 54 is frequently regarded as seminal. Symphonic concerti coexist with a large body of 'virtu-oso' concerti, which typically retain the type 5 form, albeit in Tovey's erroneous variant, and which numerically predominate in the early nineteenth century.

The notion of a dualism between 'legitimate' concerti, which collude in Mendelssohn's 'destruction' of the classical form and replace it with the 'symphonic' type 3 sonata, and an 'illegitimate' shadow repertoire, which sustain the classical paradigm in a distorted variant, is problematic for several reasons. The view of music history it promotes is essentially canonical and cleaves to a 'great man' historical model, which is at base self-justifying: Tovey's 'true concerto' is enshrined in Mozart's concerti, which fortuitously supply the evidence for the concept of the 'true con-certo'. Reasoning along these lines ensures that we maintain a distinction between canonical and non-canonical concerti: the genre proceeds from its Mozartian base, via Beethoven's initial 'mistake' and its rectification, to a small canon of legitimate contri-butions, which either avoid Mozart altogether (Mendelssohn and Schumann) or else innovate in ways that do not replicate Beethoven's misstep (Brahms). Other works, which in practice constitute the vast majority of music composed in the genre, stand outside the canon because they show no awareness of their relation-ship to Tovey's ideal type, either by fulfilment or rejection of its formal obligations.

In truth, the neat tripartition into classical (Mozartian) norms and their virtuoso and symphonic successors conceals a more complex reality. As we will see, Schumann did not perceive the field of production in this way but rather distinguished 'older' models curated, from the last decade of the eighteenth century onwards, by Field, Hummel, Chopin, Kalkbrenner, Herz, Ries, Moscheles and others, from 'new forms', exemplified in music composed after 1830 by Mendelssohn, Taubert, Moscheles and Wieck.[8] The more traditional concerti retained the type 5 sonata, but Schumann never differentiated examples depending on whether or not their first ritornello modulates; more innovative concerti departed from convention by fragmenting or dispensing with the type 5 sonata and by eliding movements or making concessions to the forms of the *Konzertstück* or 'concertino', as Schumann saw them.

Amidst all of this, Tovey's 'true concerto', enshrined in Mozart's achievement and in Beethoven's Opp. 58 and 73, played only a peripheral role. As Claudia Macdonald explains:

> From 1836 to 1840, Schumann reviewed twenty-four concertos; references to Beethoven or Mozart occur in eleven of these. They show Beethoven, and to a lesser extent Mozart, as a background presence in reviews of works Schumann championed and of ones he panned. They do not show him suggesting that modern composers return to specific older practices of these masters in the genre, nor that they take these practices as a basis for new developments. Concertos of a younger, although not the youngest, generation served this purpose instead – that is ... works by Hummel, Ries and Field.[9]

Macdonald points to Alfred Dörffel's history of the first 100 years of the Leipzig Gewandhaus concerts, which records seven performances of piano concerti by Mozart in Leipzig in the period 1831–40 and eight of concerti by Beethoven.[10] Mozart is represented by only three works in these concerts – the D minor and C minor concerti, K466 and 491, and the Double Concerto, K365 – and Beethoven by four performances of Op. 37, two of Op. 58 and two of Op. 73.[11]

Altogether, the concerti of Mozart and Beethoven were conspicuously overshadowed by virtuoso concerti in Schumann's experience during this formative period. Even as a remote ideal, Beethoven's concerti were viewed selectively by Schumann. He was especially dismissive of Op. 37, which he regarded as a tedious and uneven relic, more suitable as a museum piece for composers than a work for public consumption: 'I find much weak, much drawn out in the C minor Concerto .... The thing is to be praised, as an antiquity to be recommended to young composers; but spare the public thereby; at least use the E flat major Concerto, or the D minor of Mozart, if you offer something old.'[12] For Schumann, Beethoven was above all a composer of symphonies and masses. For concerti, Hummel, Chopin and Field provided a more reliable guide.

One consequence of this is that explaining Schumann's approach in Op. 54 in terms of a 'dialogue' with classical, Mozartian norms is hard to justify. Nothing we know about his relationship with the genre or his thinking, in advance of Op. 54's composition, about how it should progress indicates any attempt to build upon or subvert norms inherited from Mozart. If Schumann has a model, it is aggregated from the concerti of Hummel, Herz, Field, Chopin and others. This modelling is particularly overt and incontestable in the case of Herz, whose Concerto No. 1, Op. 34 served, as we will see in Chapter 3, as a template in the sketches for Schumann's unfinished Concerto of 1830–1. The ideas expressed in Schumann's critical writings of 1835–9 are direct responses to recent or contemporaneous virtuoso repertoire. Mozart is only minimally present in the genealogy of these compositions, which is more substantially indebted to practices evolving in London and Paris in the last decade of the eighteenth century, especially concerti by Dussek, Steibelt, Cramer and others.

The cleavage of nineteenth-century concerti into 'virtuoso' and 'symphonic' variants is no less problematic. The concept of the symphonic concerto has been examined in detail by Juan Martin Koch, who isolates works by Litolff, Schumann, Liszt and Brahms as its principal exponents. Identifying stable criteria for membership of this category is, however, not straightforward. The differences between pieces employing the type 5 sonata and those favouring type 3 are ostensibly clear, but many concerti attracting the symphonic label use a type 5 model in their first movement, and it is not obvious that concerti eschewing a type 5 first movement have other attributes in common which necessarily draw them closer to the symphony.

Most problematic in this respect are the five *concertos symphoniques* of Litolff, Nos. 2–5 of which were composed between 1844 and 1867 (No. 1 is lost), which are defined as such thanks primarily to their expansion of the movement cycle to include a scherzo.

In other respects, however, Litolff's concerti sit squarely in the lineage of the virtuoso concerto. All of them begin with a type 5 first movement, including (in Nos. 2, 4 and 5) a modulating ritornello, and the extrovert modes of piano writing, which Schumann disparaged in Parisian concerti by Herz and Kalkbrenner, are very much in evidence. Litolff's concerti are, moreover, not symphonic by virtue of their thematic or motivic technique. There is little value placed on motivic development or cyclical treatment of themes, and the textural integration of soloist and orchestra is largely absent. Between Litolff's symphonic concerti and Schumann's Op. 54 there is almost no obvious shared ground.

Commonalities between Juan Martin Koch's other examples are equally hard to discover. Liszt's two concerti have almost nothing in common with those of either Litolff or Schumann. His Concerto No. 1 elides two of its movements and leaves all movements formally incomplete, creating a design which, as we will explore later, Schumann considered aesthetically flawed in other similar works. And although the central movement melds a nocturne and a scherzo, any resemblance to Litolff's symphonic model ends at this point because, on the one hand, Liszt has no time for the type 5 sonata, and on the other, he is much concerned with cyclical relationships, a technique in which Litolff showed no substantive interest. The merging of sonata form and movement cycle in Liszt's Concerto No. 2, creating what Steven Vande Moortele calls a 'two-dimensional sonata', has resonances with Schumann's *Phantasie* of 1841, which subsequently became the first movement of Op. 54. Yet the rehousing of the *Phantasie* within Op. 54 somewhat diminishes the analogy, and the attitudes of Schumann and Liszt towards virtuosity could hardly be more different.

Projecting the symphonic concerto's history forward to Brahms brings its own difficulties.[13] Brahms' symphonism is most readily apparent in Op. 83, which obviously invokes Litolff's symphonic concerti in its inclusion of a scherzo. Yet both Op. 15 and Op. 83 depart fundamentally from Schumann's precedent because they revive the type 5 sonata, albeit in Op. 15 through the presence of a single, very large opening ritornello. Brahms' pianism is economical in ways that owe far more to Schumann than to Litolff, but the overt monumentality of Brahms's style, which in the case of

17

Op. 15 tracks explicitly to the work's origins as a symphony, resembles neither Schumann, nor Litolff, nor Liszt. In sum, although links to the symphony can be made plausibly for all these works, their only common denominator as a group is a habitual separation, in reception history, from the virtuoso concerto.

An Alternative Model

Doing historical and analytical justice to Schumann's Op. 54 consequently requires us to think in fresh ways about the development of the piano concerto in the early nineteenth century. In particular, a primary orientation around Mozart and Beethoven is neither analytically helpful nor historically defensible. Of far more significance for Op. 54 is Schumann's critical reaction to contemporaneous concerti seeking to innovate beyond the virtuoso variant of the type 5 sonata and the ways in which his Concerto realises formal, textural and expressive alternatives. The symphony is, to be sure, a factor in the formulation of Schumann's approach, but neither the details of Op. 54's technique, nor its angle of relation to the virtuoso concerto, nor any similarities with other 'symphonic' concerti allow us to make neat distinctions between Hummel, Field, Kalkbrenner, Chopin and Herz, on the one hand, and Schumann, Liszt and Litolff on the other.

It is more constructive to situate Schumann's Op. 54 within a general, post-classical concerted practice, which is orientated around a cosmopolitan repertoire stemming from the concerti of Dussek, Steibelt and Cramer, inter alia, in the last decade of the eighteenth century, as the ultimate source of Schumann's 'old forms'. This diversifies in the 1830s and 1840s to encompass a wide variety of novel designs and incorporates forms that customarily mark other genres, including the symphony. Cutting across all of this is a shared vocabulary of pianistic and concerted style, which is evident throughout the repertoire and remains operative into the late nineteenth and early twentieth centuries. The problem of how to write for two combined media – the piano and the orchestra – which seem complete in themselves is at the heart of Schumann's approach and supplies a more secure starting point from which to comprehend his innovations. This in turn suggests that the forms of the Romantic concerto are better grasped as vehicles for the articulation of pianistic style than as imperfect responses to Mozart or expressions of a dialectic of virtuosity and symphonism, even though these two concepts significantly influence the repertoire.

Virtuosity

Above all, a substantial understanding of Schumann's Concerto requires an approach that takes due account of early nineteenth-century virtuosity. By the second decade of the nineteenth century, a lexicon of piano styles had emerged which is foundational not only to the ways in which composers write for the instrument in a concerted context but also to the evolution of concerto forms.[14] This practice coalesced into a model of virtuosity, the elements of which, following Leonard Ratner's definition as 'subjects for musical discourse', elaborated by Danuta Mirka as '*musical styles and genres taken out of their proper context and used in another one*', I will call *topics*.[15] Specifically, concerted virtuosity relied on a threefold division of labour into bravura, cantabile and *brillante* or display topics.[16]

The features of this tripartition are neatly compartmentalised in the first-movement solo entry of Kalkbrenner's Concerto No. 4, Op. 127 (1835), quoted in Example 1.1. The pianist enters in bar 21 with expansive gestures, in which thick chordal textures and elaborative flourishes predominate. At bar 30, this gives way to a very different stylistic milieu, characterised by a flowing, continuous left-hand accompaniment supporting an ornately embellished right-hand melody. This new section closes with a perfect authentic cadence or PAC in bar 45, and a transition (TR) begins, which is texturally different again, swapping the dense ornamentation of bars 30–44 for continuous semiquaver figuration.[17] I will refer to the extrovert style of bars 21–9 as a *bravura topic*; adopting Hepokoski and Darcy's terminology, I will call the soloist's initial material a 'preface'. Combined, they produce a *bravura preface*: a solo incipit, which mingles dense chordal writing, double-octave passagework and rapid but intermittent scalar or

Example 1.1 Kalkbrenner, Piano Concerto No. 4, Op. 127, first movement, first theme and start of transition.

arpeggiated flourishes.[18] The texture emerging from bar 30 owes more to the melody-and-accompaniment singing style of the late eighteenth century, which typically distributes the pianist's labour between sustained accompanimental figuration in the left hand and melodic declamation in the right, for which reason I term it a *cantabile episode*. By the 1830s, this style had come to be associated predominantly with the nocturne, thanks primarily to Field and subsequently to Chopin, but its origins are apparent in music of the so-called London pianoforte school composed in the last decade of the eighteenth century and in the context of the concerto, especially Dussek, with whose music Field was much engaged in the years prior to Field's permanent departure from London to Russia in 1802.[19] Cantabile episodes, in brief, often invoke a *nocturne topic*, which is distinguishable from the classical singing style by the wide left-hand tessitura enabling the separation of bass from interior voices, made possible by advances in sustaining-pedal technology.[20] Finally, the continuous semi-quaver patterns of Kalkbrenner's transition reference the *brillante* style, and as a topic are generally associated with display, a demonstration of technical facility emphasising the execution of sustained rather than spasmodic passagework.[21]

The ubiquity of the bravura preface's conventions is made apparent by Example 1.2, which quotes instances by Dussek, Field, Ries, Herz, Moscheles and Chopin. In each case, the composer exploits the same stylistic ingredients. The preface begins with a chordal or octave incipit. In Dussek's Op. 22, Field's No. 4, Ries' Op. 42, Herz's Op. 34 and Moscheles' Op. 45, this gesture is standardised to the point of conventionality: three or four widely spaced chords serve as a call to order, which is followed by a scalar or arpeggiated flourish. Chopin's Op. 11 is more complex because the octave incipit is motivic, recalling the head motive of the ritornello's first theme. But Chopin then falls in line with virtuoso practice by embellishing his incipit with rapid arpeggiated figuration.

Cantabile episodes are in one sense more diverse in that their initiating material is less highly conventionalised; the passage from bravura preface to cantabile continuation is nonetheless easy to detect. Example 1.3 provides instances by Dussek (Op. 22), Steibelt (No. 4), Field (No. 7), Herz (Op. 34 again), Kalkbrenner (No. 3) and Chopin (Op. 11 again), spanning 1793 to 1832. Field and Herz both deploy a left-hand texture that is clearly an offspring of the Alberti bass, consisting of sextuplet arpeggiations displaced from a registrally distinct bass. This texture's genealogy is readily

Example 1.2 Bravura prefaces in Dussek, Op. 22; Field, Concerto No. 4; Ries, Op. 42; Herz, Op. 34; Moscheles, Op. 45; and Chopin, Op. 11.

apparent if we look at Steibelt's Concerto No. 3 and Dussek's Op. 22, the cantabile episodes of which are underpinned by more obviously classical Alberti figuration. Kalkbrenner and Chopin make use of an alternative but equally common texture, which

An Alternative Model

Example 1.2 (cont.)

displaces a bass line from a repeated or arpeggiated chordal texture. The singing melody above these textures becomes increasingly decorative over time, culminating in the dense fioritura employed

Example 1.3 Cantabile episodes in Dussek, Steibelt, Field, Herz, Kalkbrenner and Chopin.

by Kalkbrenner and Chopin. The chronological progression of the excerpts in Example 1.3 is clear in this respect. Field's style, which reflects his seminal role in the development of the piano nocturne as a genre between 1800 and 1830, mediates between Dussek and

Example 1.3 (cont.)

Steibelt on the one hand, who are active in the 1790s and 1800s, and Herz, Kalkbrenner and Chopin on the other, whose concerti date from 1828, 1829 and 1830, respectively.

Composers devised varied ways of moving from the cantabile episode into the display TR. In the cases of Field's Concerto No. 7, Chopin's Op. 11 and Kalkbrenner's Concerto No. 4, the cantabile episode reaches a tonic PAC and the display episode begins as a clearly defined new section. Kalkbrenner's No. 3 and Herz's No. I are less straightforward. In the former, the modulatory labour of the TR is begun by the cantabile episode, and the nocturne style dissolves into an amalgam of bravura and *brillante* topics as soon as the music reaches V/III in anticipation of the second theme. In the latter, the TR is demarcated by a clear tonic PAC but the cantabile episode tends increasingly towards a bravura style, which is fully recovered as TR approaches. Hummel's Concerto No. 2, Op. 85, excerpted in Example 1.4, is more complex again. Hummel's solo entry eschews the bravura extroversion of Herz and Kalkbrenner in favour of music recalling the sensibility style or *Empfindsamkeit* associated with C. P. E. Bach, stabilising in the singing style with the theme's continuation phrase at bar 132. Hummel closes this phrase with a tonic PAC at bar 139 and appears to move directly into a display TR. But this music fails to modulate, and a further tonic PAC in bar 152 ushers in a second cantabile episode, which now undertakes the modulatory labour that the display material had failed to secure. *Brillante* figuration returns as soon as V/III is reached, and the transition concludes in an orthodox manner with a dominant prolongation presaging the second theme, sustained by elaborate right-hand passagework. Hummel was equally inventive in his Concerto No. 3, Op. 89, in which the cantabile episode expands to encompass the entire solo entry, breaking into display as the cadence signalling the TR approaches. The bravura style is then reserved for the TR's start, which follows in the piano after a short tutti referencing the orchestra's first theme.

The interaction of soloist and orchestra further complicates this picture. Typically, the orchestra's material employs and augments a topical lexicon inherited from the late eighteenth century: first themes are often martial; second themes exemplify the singing style; transitions and closing sections mobilise *tempesta* or *ombra* topics or incorporate underpinning *Trommelbass* patterns. Here again, Field is exemplary. His orchestral first themes divide into

An Alternative Model

Example 1.4 Hummel, Op. 85/i, S1 A theme preface, cantabile and display episodes.

two topical categories: Nos. 1, 3 and 6 are patently martial; 2 and 4 are more reflective and might profitably be defined as *espressivo* first themes. Indeed, No. 2 could be said to supply the paradigm of the *espressivo* concerto first theme, consolidating a style that is

Example 1.5 Field, Concerto No. 7/I, R1 B theme.

periodically replicated, sometimes in conjunction with the key of A flat as well; Ferdinand Hiller's *Concerto espressivo*, Op. 170 of 1874, also in A flat, offers an instructive comparison. Field's Concerto No. 7 sits somewhere between the two: its mournful C minor first theme is really a processional march in $\frac{3}{4}$ time, the solemnity of which is enhanced by the initial timpani rolls and pizzicato walking bass. Field's orchestral second themes are sometimes cantabile topics (Nos. 4, 5 and 6) and sometimes begin life as marches but shade into the singing style (Nos. 2, 3 and 7). Concerto No. 7, quoted in Example 1.5, shows this clearly. The theme opens in bar 56 with music that projects martial characteristics, notably in its dotted rhythms; with the cadence in bars 63–4, however, the topic shifts identifiably to the singing style, evident in the legato melody and flowing quaver accompaniment.

As Chapter 2 will explore, Schumann was a keen student of the styles and techniques of the virtuoso concerto. But although he frequently responded critically to virtuosity's conventions, his approach in Op. 54 is not to reject them but to redeploy them as the textural interior of a concerted style, which fused virtuosity with other stylistic and generic markers.

Lyricism

As Dahlhaus observes, Op. 54 is also significantly indebted to the Romantic character piece, an association that brings with it quite different aesthetic and social implications: if Schumann's interest in virtuosity and the concerti that served as its vehicle inform Op. 54's public dimension, then resonances with the Romantic character piece point instead to a private, domestic sphere, which is no less influential on his concerted style.[22] Moreover, when Dahlhaus affiliates this mode of pianism with lyricism, he has in mind a dichotomy between drama and poetry, which is often framed in terms of the differences between the music of Beethoven and Schubert: sonata-type genres, especially the symphony, enact an allegory of dramatic action; songs are vehicles for text-setting, which means they cleave to the rhetoric of poetry rather than drama; and piano miniatures mimic songs in their aesthetic aspirations, but wordlessly, such that their musical rhetoric is lyrical rather than dramatic, even though no poetic text is explicitly referenced.[23] Dahlhaus' description of Op. 54's first movement as 'a piano piece with orchestral accompaniment' steers the work away from virtuosity altogether, proposing instead that it is, in effect, a character piece writ large.

If the lyric miniature has any clear point of origin, then it is surely Field's nocturnes. Field's innovation was recognised by Liszt, for whom Field's nocturnes played a crucial music-historical role because they were the first examples of a musical form unfettered by eighteenth-century conventions. As Liszt argued: 'we owe [to Field] the first essays which feeling and revery ventured to make on the piano, to free themselves from the constraints exercised over them by the regular and official model imposed until that time on all compositions'.[24] Field achieved this by reanimating a device that harks back to the baroque prelude, which is the establishment of a uniform accompanimental keyboard figuration as the textural basis of an entire piece. The Nocturne No. 1, the opening of which is given in Example 1.6, is exemplary. The left-hand figure, which is clearly an evolution of the classical Alberti bass, persists for the piece's duration, allowing Field to build a freely elaborated cantabile melody above. The same idea permeates Mendelssohn's *Songs without Words* (*Lieder ohne Worte*), the generic title of which makes their lyric rather than dramatic associations overt. Mendelssohn's Op. 19, No. 1, the opening of which is quoted in Example 1.7, develops beyond Field's example in that its invariant

Example 1.6 Field, Nocturne No. 1, H24.

Example 1.7 Mendelssohn, *Lieder ohne Worte*, Op. 19, No. 1.

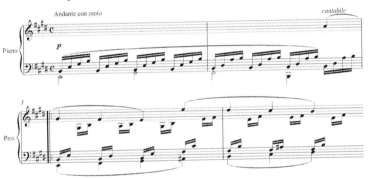

figuration is now distributed as the music's interior, thereby supplying the alto and tenor voices inside an explicit soprano-bass framework.

These techniques acquired new levels of subtlety and sophistication in the music of Chopin and Schumann, whose contributions differ in that Schumann preferred to assemble his character pieces into cycles defined by an overarching literary or poetic theme, whereas Chopin, with the sovereign exception of the Op. 28 Preludes, simply published them in small generic groups under a single opus number. Consequently, in Schumann's hands, the lyric character piece served a more ambitious extra-musical agenda, which was to express an overarching quasi-novelistic meaning. Daverio cites this habit as central to Schumann's aesthetic across all genres; for him, Schumann's aim was to imbue music 'with the same intellectual substance as literature', a goal he pursued, in the piano cycles of the 1830s, by treating collections of character pieces as 'systems of fragments', which together formed a novelistic whole that is more than the sum of its parts.[25] The lyric affiliations of Schumann's piano miniatures are further reinforced because, from 1840, he deployed their textures in the composition of songs as well, again in contrast with Chopin. Compare, for example, the postludes to the Arabesque, Op. 18 and *Dichterliebe*, Op. 48, which employ near-identical textures and with similar valedictory expressive intent.

Field supplies a clear link between the character piece and the concerto, adopting the former's manner both within concerto movements and sometimes as their defining characteristic. The slow movement of his Concerto No. 2, a work that persisted in the repertoire for much of the nineteenth century, is a piano nocturne pure and simple, to which Field adds a light, supporting orchestral accompaniment. Field went further in his Concerto No. 7, incorporating a self-standing nocturne between the end of the first movement's exposition and the beginning of the development, which he also published independently as the Nocturne No. 12. As we discover once the rondo second movement begins, the interpolated nocturne *is* in fact the slow movement, now reconceived as a lyric episode within the first movement.

Schumann's response to this passage in his essay on the work for the *Neue Zeitschrift für Musik* evidences the extent to which his conceptions of the concerto and the lyric character piece were entangled, both with each other and with his literary imagination. His description of Field's first-movement episode as 'a moonlight nocturne "woven of rose dust and lily snow"' misquotes Canto IV, Stanza 6 of Christoph Martin Wieland's epic poem *Oberon*, which narrates the Paladin's encounter with his first love in a 'dream story': the opening lines of the stanza read: 'Think of a woman in the purest youthful light / After an archetype from above / Woven of rose glow and lily snow' (*Denk dir ein Weib im reinsten Jugendlicht / Nach einem Urbild von dort oben / Aus Rosengluth und Lilienschnee gewoben*).[26] As I, Juan Martin Koch and others have noted, and as will be investigated in more detail in Chapter 3, this passage in Field's Concerto is one tangible model for the *andante espressivo* in the first movement of Op. 54, which appears at the same formal location, deploys the same topic and has a similar expressive effect.

Dahlhaus' insistence that Op. 54 is in essence a lyric concerto surely underestimates the formative influence of virtuosity on Schumann's concept of the genre; his conclusion that 'to proclaim [Op. 54] . . . as the prototype of the symphonic concerto' is 'misleading' also overstates the case, since it leaves unexplained the work's thematic economy of means and cyclical motivic techniques. The lyric character piece is better understood as an important additional source of pianistic topics that Schumann exploits, which had begun to infuse the forms of the piano concerto before he came to the genre.

Form

When Tovey differentiated Mozart's 'true' concerto principle from the fallacious alternative propagated by virtuoso composers, he objected above all to the presence of a modulating first ritornello. Writ large, however, this repertoire's first movements articulate a form, which is different from Mozart's practice in several respects. Any evaluation of the virtuoso concerto and Schumann's response to it consequently requires us to account for its full range of formal strategies, which, *pace* Tovey, do not originate with Beethoven and are not significantly influenced by him.

Building on the work of Isabella Amster, John Rink has identified an 'archetype' for the virtuoso type 5 sonata, explained in Table 1.1.[27] Rink defines a seven-part scheme, in which the three solo episodes (S_1, S_2 and S_3) project exposition, development and recapitulation functions, respectively. S_1 comprises two themes, both of which are succeeded by a *Spielepisode* or display episode, which is distinctive by virtue of its focus on *brillante* virtuosity and is conceived with a principle of melodic contrast in mind that, in Jim Samson's terms, pits display against 'poetry'.[28] This pattern is replicated in S_3, except that the material remains in the tonic; and the second display episode takes on the character of an operatic cabaletta or 'finale', conceived, as Rink explains, 'to build excitement' in anticipation of the movement's end. S_2 also divides into poetic and virtuosic sub-sections and

Table 1.1 *Rink/Amster model of the virtuoso type 5 sonata*

Sonata form analogue:	Exposition				---	Development		---	Recapitulation			Coda	
Thematic group/section:	theme 1	Spielepisode 1	theme 2	Spielepisode 2		new theme?	virtuosity		theme 1	Spielepisode 1	theme 2	'finale'	
Tutti/solo:	T_1	S_1				T_2	S_2		T_3	S_3			T_4
Main key:	I	→	new key (e.g. III, V)			→V			I				

may or may not be developmental of S_1's material. The orchestral tuttis (T_1, T_2, T_3 and T_4 in Rink's terminology) punctuate the sonata functions: T_1 serves to introduce 'the principal themes in preparation for the first solo'; T_2 rounds off the exposition and prepares S_2; T_3 closes the development; and T_4 functions as a coda.

Comparison of Rink's type 5 archetype with Hepokoski and Darcy's Mozartian alternative reveals similarities and differences. The virtuoso variant retains basic classical formal markers, including the medial caesura (MC), which is the cadential or half-cadential pause articulating the end of the transition and start of the second theme in the solo exposition and recapitulation, as well as the structural cadence that defines the end of the expositional second theme, which Hepokoski and Darcy call the 'essential expositional closure' or EEC, and its transposition into the tonic in the recapitulation, generating the 'essential structural closure' or ESC.[29] On the other hand, Ritornello 1 (R1; Rink's T_1) modulates more often than not, presenting its second theme in whole or part in a non-tonic key.[30] There are also striking differences between Mozart's first solo episodes (S1) and those of the virtuoso repertoire. Mozart invariably employs R1's first theme (R1 A in my terminology) at or near the start of S1 (that is, R1 A and S1 A are the same theme) but provides the soloist with a different second or B theme (R1 B and S1 B are not the same), whereas in virtuoso first movements, R1 and S1 will share a B theme but not an A theme. These features respond directly to the distinctive formal implications of non-modulating and modulating R1s: Mozart provides new music for S1 B in order to articulate the B-theme modulation; in virtuoso concerti, S1 B reproduces R1 B's modulation and consequently its theme as well. These differences have implications for the recapitulation. In his later concerti, Mozart sometimes uses the recapitulation as an opportunity to synthesise R1 and S1 by reprising the B themes of both in the tonic (K. 491 and K. 503 exemplify this clearly). In the virtuoso concerto, the recapitulation is more likely to start with a reprise of R1 A, often as R3, and the soloist intervenes somewhere in the later form-functional course of A or TR; and the B theme shared between R1 and S1 now returns in the tonic. Finally, Mozart always bisects R4 with a cadenza, a practice that dies out almost completely in the virtuoso repertoire. Dussek, for example, never writes cadenzas, and in subsequent repertoire they are sporadically present and sometimes moved to different formal locations.

Relating these observations to the issues of topical discourse considered earlier produces the form described in Table 1.2. Crucially, form and topic are precisely correlated. The threefold model that operates in S1 A and TR (bravura preface; cantabile episode; display transition) is replicated at a higher formal level: the contrast between S1 B and the closing section (C), S3 B and C and the first two sections of the development (which I call the pre-core and core, following William Caplin) is also a contrast between cantabile and display topics.[31] The solo regions of the form are, above all, vehicles for the articulation of these topical contrasts, which are also the soloist's expressive subject positions: extroversion, in the twin forms of bravura and *brillante*; and intimacy in the cantabile episodes. The form, in effect, offers a platform for the material and tonal mediation of the soloist's public and private personas.

As we will see in Chapter 2 and explore in more detail in Chapter 3, a central feature of Schumann's attitude to the genre is his abandonment of this scheme, which in the hands of Parisian virtuosi especially served to exacerbate the separation of piano and orchestra. As with virtuosity's threefold topical discourse, however, so also with its forms, Schumann did not reject the virtuoso type 5 precedent entirely but rather subsumed many of its ingredients into a 'type 3' sonata. His approach, in short, is more concerned with sublimating the virtuoso model than with rejecting it.

Texture, Dialogue and Society

When Schumann complained, in a review for the *Neue Zeitschrift für Musik*, that the first movement of Kalkbrenner's Concerto No. 4, Op. 127 alternated between solo and orchestral music without any obvious concern for their interaction, he raised an issue that is textural as well as formal and topical: the piano requires minimal support from the orchestra and vice versa, for which reason their integration is neither a significant feature of the music nor a concern of the composer. The challenge Schumann set

Table 1.2 *Bravura-nocturne-display model mapped onto virtuoso type 5 sonata form*

R/S succession:	R1				S1				R2
Sonata form:	exposition 1				exposition 2				
	A	TR	B	C	A	TR	B	C	
Topic:	e.g. march	*Trommelbass/tempesta*	singing style	march/*Trommelbass/tempesta*	bravura–singing style (nocturne)	*Brillante* (display episode)	singing style (nocturne)	*Brillante* (display episode)	march/*Trommelbass/tempesta*
Key:	I or I		V or III→	I or i; or V or III→I or i	I or i	↑	V or III		
Cadence:	PAC		MC	PAC	PAC	MC		PAC	

R/S succession:	S2		R3	S3				R4
Sonata form:	development		retransition (RT)	recapitulation				coda
	pre-core	core		A	TR	B	C	
Topic:	singing style (nocturne)	*Brillante* (display episode)		e.g. march; bravura–singing style (nocturne)	*Brillante* (display episode)	singing style (nocturne)	*Brillante* (display episode)	march/*Trommelbass/tempesta*
Key:	various keys		↑	I or i				
Cadence:	PAC or HC	HC		PAC	MC		PAC	

for himself was, in part, to work out how the two might be integrated without impairing their mutual self-sufficiency. This is, in no small measure, a matter of texture, and more specifically of the types of *concertante* writing that the pianist and orchestra might collectively generate. Schumann's point is that Kalkbrenner's response to this challenge fails aesthetically because it does not posit an instrumental milieu in which soloist and orchestra need each other, with the consequence that the orchestra comes to seem redundant.

The complaint of orchestral redundancy has been most frequently and persistently levelled at Chopin. In the first movement of his Concerto Op. 21, the orchestral accompaniment is restricted to the strings alone for almost the entire duration of S1: the first horn interjects for three bars during the first-theme group cantabile episode, and the horns and upper winds return for S1's last two bars, fleshing out the texture supporting the soloist's cadential trill. The winds are more actively involved in S2, but generally as soloists or in groups of two or three. Solo 3 is no more orchestrally diverse than S1: the strings accompany throughout; horn 1 plays for four bars during the transition into the second theme, and again with a single held note midway through the closing section; and horns, clarinets and timpani add to the texture as the pianist's final cadential trill cedes to R4.

The point, of course, is not that Chopin's orchestral writing is inadequate but that his piano writing obviates the need for more substantive orchestral involvement. In this respect, it is telling that the winds are most engaged during the development section (S2), where they supply first-theme motivic material against the soloist's display figuration: that is to say, they are deployed when the thematic material cannot be accommodated by the piano. To this extent, the aesthetic of Chopin's Op. 21 is self-consistent and grounded in the idea that piano concerti should give their solo instrument an opportunity to unfold its full textural potential. In this respect, his attitude is of a piece with Kalkbrenner and the virtuoso tradition more generally. The first movement of Hummel's Op. 85, a work that had a pivotal influence on Schumann, is hardly different. Hummel also restricts his orchestral accompaniment almost entirely to the strings during S1, excepting one passage in the second theme between bars 194 and 206, where they are replaced by the winds. The entirety of the display-episode closing section is supported by strings alone, and often more sparsely than in Chopin's Op. 21; and Hummel also dovetails S1 and R2 by reintroducing the winds over the soloist's ultimate dominant. Hummel's development section is even more orchestrally cautious than Chopin's: in the whole of its eighty-two bars, the winds play for only nine, and then predominantly as soloists; and the horns enter only in the final two bars of the retransition.

In his work on Mozart's piano concerti, Simon Keefe has emphasised the notion of dramatic dialogue as essential to Mozart's approach.[32] For Keefe, Mozart's concerti dramatise modes of dialogue in line with contemporary accounts of the genre, notably those of Heinrich Christoph Koch, Kollmann and Reicha, for whom the essence of the concerto resides in the dual meaning of the verb *concertare*, as 'compete' or 'contend' (in Latin) and 'agree' or 'collaborate' (in Italian). Keefe identifies parallels in late-eighteenth-century ideas of drama, drawing out instances in Mozart's concerti where these two conflicting concepts define the relationship between soloist and orchestra in analogy with spoken drama. Hummel, Chopin, Kalkbrenner and others aim at a fundamentally different idea: the purpose of the solo episodes in their concerti is not to place pianist and orchestra in conflict, collaboration or mediation but to unfold the soloist's own material, topical and textural contrasts, which the orchestra discretely facilitates. As Rink avers, the early nineteenth century was more concerned with principles of alternation than conflict, collaboration or synthesis, an inclination he relates to the expressive concerns of grand opera.[33] Viewed in these terms, the orchestral modesty of virtuoso solo expositions provides a platform for the soloist's oscillation of topical, expressive subject positions addressed earlier. On the largest scale, this alternation also articulates the form: the orchestra enters and comments, once the soloist's discourse has been completed within a given large-scale formal span.

Keefe, however, goes further, contending that Mozart's attitude towards concerted dialogue reflects its social context. Mozart's concerti sought an ultimate state of cooperation via a series of dramatic twists and turns in the relationship between soloist and orchestra, which he challenged the listener to follow and absorb. As Keefe asserts: 'By engaging his listener in a challenging intellectual pursuit, Mozart offered him or her an excellent vehicle for learning about cooperation (or, more precisely, the quest for cooperation), a value deeply cherished in the Age of Enlightenment. Mozart's concertos thus fulfilled the single most important requirement for all late-eighteenth-century music and drama: the general instruction of the listener-spectator.'[34]

Virtuoso concerti can be similarly construed, except to say that the relationship between individual and collective has changed fundamentally. In place of the Enlightenment notion of rational dialogue to the end of collaborative action, virtuoso concerti offer a sharp contrast between individual and collective, in which the former is elevated to a condition of self-sufficiency. The orchestra's relatively passive involvement in the soloist's material suggests that the duty of the collective is to subordinate itself to the individual, the expression of whose subjective-poetic condition it is the genre's principal duty to convey.

Critics frequently complained about the narcissistic and ultimately pecuniary agenda that this generic concept served, given that virtuoso concerti were invariably composed by virtuosi to advance their careers.[35] Behind this, however, lurks a more fundamental difference between Enlightenment and Romantic values. The ideal that virtuosity embodies is one of radical individualism, indebted more to Hegel than to Kant, central to which is a conception of the artist as a world-historical, heroic protagonist. In all of the examples we have considered, the soloist's expressive world is never challenged by the orchestra, which rather resembles a crowd that falls silent when the virtuoso speaks and only comments when their discourse is paused or completed. To this extent, the soloist's dramatic discourse is a reflexive, not a collective conversation, which is voiced by the alternation of topics and subject positions and articulated by the type 5 sonata form.

Schumann's turn to a type 3 sonata in Op. 54's first movement consequently has deep implications for the genre's mode of social discourse and by extension for the political order with which the music affiliates. As Chapter 3 argues, the *Phantasie*'s integration of soloist and orchestra responds not only to a critique of generic practices but more fundamentally to the social order of which those practices are allegorical. In an important sense, Schumann's Piano Concerto realises a strain of political idealism in musical form.

Notes

1. James Hepokoski and Warren Darcy, *Elements of Sonata Theory: Norms, Types, and Deformations in the Late-Eighteenth-Century Sonata* (New York: Oxford University Press, 2006), 430–602.
2. Donald Francis Tovey, 'LXXXV: The Classical Concerto', in *Essays in Musical Analysis, Vol. 3, Concertos* (London: Oxford University Press, 1936, repr. 1948), 3–27.
3. Ibid., 3.
4. Tovey, 'C: Beethoven, Pianoforte Concerto in C Major, Op. 15', *Essays in Musical Analysis, Vol. 3*, 64–9, at 64.
5. Tovey, 'CXX: Mendelssohn, Violin Concerto in E Minor, Op. 64', *Essays in Musical Analysis, Vol. 3*, 178–81, at 178.
6. Tovey, 'CXXI: Schumann, Pianoforte Concerto in A Minor, Op. 54', *Essays in Musical Analysis, Vol. 3*, 182–4, at 182.
7. Hepokoski and Darcy, *Elements of Sonata Theory*, 434.
8. Macdonald, *Robert Schumann and the Piano Concerto*, 91–134.
9. Ibid., 75.
10. Alfred Dörffel, *Statistik der Concerte im Saale des Gewandhause zu Leipzig, 25 November 1781–25 November 1881* (Leipzig: Breitkopf und Härtel, 1881), 6 (Beethoven's concerti) and 43 (Mozart's concerti).
11. Macdonald records one performance of Beethoven's Op. 37 by Camilla Pleyel on 2 November 1839, which does not appear on Dörffel's list. See *Robert Schumann and the Piano Concerto*, 79.
12. Ibid., 89, translated from Bodo Bischoff and Gerd Nauhaus, 'Robert Schumanns Leipziger Konzertnotizen von 1833: Faksimile, Übertragung und Kommentar (Erstveröffentlichung)', *Schumann-Studien 3/4* (1994): 45.
13. For detailed consideration of Brahms' response to these issues, see Julian Horton, *Brahms's Piano Concerto No. 2, Op. 83: Analytical and Contextual Studies* (Leuven: Peeters, 2017).
14. For a detailed study of the piano's evolution and repertoire between 1760 and 1850, see Derek Carew, *The Mechanical Muse: The Piano, Pianism and Piano Music, c. 1760–1850* (Aldershot: Ashgate, 2007); on the aesthetics of virtuoso pianism, see Jim Samson, *Virtuosity and the Musical Work: The Transcendental Studies of*

Liszt (Cambridge: Cambridge University Press, 2003). On the tradition of Romantic pianism orientated around Liszt, see Kenneth Hamilton, *After the Golden Age* (New York: Oxford University Press, 2007).

15. Leonard Ratner, *Classic Music: Expression, Form, and Style* (New York: Schirmer, 1980), 9 and 'Introduction', in Danuta Mirka, ed., *The Oxford Handbook of Topic Theory* (New York: Oxford University Press, 2014), 2, italics in original.

16. On the threefold model of virtuoso topics, see, for example, Julian Horton, 'Formal Type and Formal Function in the Post-Classical Piano Concerto', in Julie Pedneault-Deslauriers, Nathan John Martin and Steven Vande Moortele, eds., *Formal Functions in Perspective: Essays in Musical Form from Haydn to Adorno* (Rochester, NY: University of Rochester Press, 2015), 77–122, at 90–9. My model has been elaborated by Margaret Fox, who interprets the bravura preface as a transplantation of cadenza-like elements into the soloist's exposition in lieu of a cadenza in its classical location (bisecting R4). Fox reads this as a musical application of Friedrich Schlegel's concept of the arabesque, in which traditionally ornamental features (*Beiwerk*) become integrated into the main formal discourse (*Hauptwerk*). See Margaret Elizabeth Fox, 'Deciphering the Arabesque: Genre Mixture and Formal Digression in the Early Romantic Piano Concerto' (PhD dissertation: University of Toronto, 2021), 46–7 and 55–65.

17. My terminology for cadences follows that of William Caplin. Authentic cadences conclude with a V–I progression. If the soprano voice above this falls to the tonic scale degree, then we have a perfect authentic cadence or PAC; if it does not, then we have an imperfect authentic cadence or IAC. I call cadential progressions terminating on V half-cadences (HC) and on vi or VI deceptive cadences (DC). I call an authentic cadence, the tonic of resolution of which is withheld or qualified, an 'evaded' cadence and cadential progressions that disperse before their dominant is properly asserted 'abandoned' cadences. See William E. Caplin, 'The Classical Cadence: Conceptions and Misconceptions', *Journal of the American Musicological Society* 57/1 (2004): 51–118 and also 'Beyond the Classical Cadence: Thematic Closure in Early Romantic Music', *Music Theory Spectrum* 40/1 (2018): 1–26.

18. On the varieties of solo-entry preface in Mozart's concerti, see Hepokoski and Darcy, *Elements of Sonata Theory*, 498–520.

19. On the development of the nocturne, see Nicholas Temperley, 'John Field and the First Nocturne', *Music & Letters* 56/3–4 (1975): 335–40. The genesis of Field's early nocturnes is an uncertain subject. Their origins predate the first publications by some time and he

considered alternative titles for many of the pieces finally published under this name, including romance, pastoral and serenade. Temperley states that, prior to the publication of the Dalmas edition of Field's Nocturne No. 1 in 1812, 'the word had not been used before, as far as I know, for a piece for solo piano' (ibid., 337). Temperley also traces the origins of the style to the evolution of the sustaining pedal and its capacity to maintain a bass line more than an octave beneath the left-hand accompaniment; see 337–40. On this subject, see also Majella Boland, 'John Field in Context: A Reappraisal of the Nocturnes and Piano Concerti' (PhD dissertation: University College Dublin, 2013).

20. The development of the split damper pedal allowing the player to lift the damper in one half of the keyboard but not the other, as employed, for example, in the piano that Broadwood provided for Beethoven in 1817, is particularly germane to this style, since it allows for sustained textures in the left hand to coexist with damped melodies in the right. On the development of piano pedalling in this period, see David Rowland, *A History of Pianoforte Pedalling* (Cambridge: Cambridge University Press, 1993), 17–25.

21. The *brillante* or 'brilliant' style is defined by Leonard Ratner as 'the use of rapid passages for virtuoso display or intense feeling'; see *Classic Music: Expression, Form and Style* (New York: Schirmer, 1980), 19. For a more recent consideration of the 'brilliant' style, see Roman Ivanovich, 'The Brilliant Style', in Danuta Mirka, ed., *The Oxford Handbook of Topic Theory*, 330–54.

22. On musical intimacy and the public and private spheres in the nineteenth century, see Wolfgang Fuhrmann, 'The Intimate Art of Listening: Music in the Private Sphere during the Nineteenth Century', in Christian Thorau and Hansjakob Ziemer, eds., *The Oxford Handbook of Music Listening in the Nineteenth and Twentieth Centuries* (New York: Oxford University Press, 2019), 284–311.

23. On the lyric in Schubert's instrumental music, see Su-Yin Mak, 'Schubert's Sonata Forms and the Poetics of the Lyric', *Journal of Musicology* 23/2 (2006): 263–306.

24. Franz Liszt, 'Prämium-Beigabe zu John Field, Nocturnes', translated by Julius Schuberth in Franz Liszt, ed., *John Field: 18 Nocturnes* (J. Schuberth: Leipzig, 1859), 1–8, at 5.

25. Daverio, *Robert Schumann*, 19. The concept of the Romantic fragment traces back to Friedrich Schlegel, *Athenaeumsfragment*, 116; see Friedrich Schlegel, *Philosophical Fragments*, translated by Peter Firchow (Minneapolis: University of Minnesota Press, 1991). On Schumann and the Romantic fragment, see also John Daverio, 'Schumann's System of Musical Fragments and *Witz*', in

Nineteenth-Century Music and the German Romantic Ideology
(New York: Schirmer, 1993), 49–88 and Nathan John Martin,
'Schumann's Fragment', *Indiana Theory Review* 28/1–2 (2010):
85–109.

26. Schumann's misquotation reads 'aus Rosendust und Lilienschnee
gewoben'; see *Neue Zeitschrift für Musik* 4/29 (8 April 1836): 122.
I am grateful to Nicole Grimes for pointing out the connection with
Wieland's poem.

27. John Rink, *Chopin: The Piano Concertos* (Cambridge: Cambridge
University Press, 1997), 3–6 and Isabella Amster, *Das Virtuosen-
konzert in der ersten Hälfte des 19. Jahrhunderts* (Wolfenbüttel:
Kallmeyer, 1931).

28. Jim Samson, *The Music of Chopin* (Oxford: Clarendon Press, 1994),
29, referring to Chopin's Op. 21: 'The pianist carries us with him
through a succession of impulsively changing roles – showman,
combatant, poet – with an engaging spontaneity denied to the sonata
or symphony.'

29. See *Elements of Sonata Theory*, 16–20, 120–31 (on the EEC) and
232–3 (on the ESC).

30. As I have shown elsewhere, there are five common R1 variants in
virtuoso concerti: (1) R1 modulates for its second theme (B) and
coordinates a return to the tonic with a reprise of the first theme (A),
sometimes followed by a closing section (C), generating a ritornello
that has strong ternary characteristics. (2) R1 modulates for its
B theme, cadences in the new key and then returns to the tonic for
a C section. (3) R1 modulates for its B theme, but this theme returns
to the tonic during its course, closing with a cadence that ushers in
a tonic C section. (4) R1 modulates for its B theme, but a subsequent
return to the tonic is only completed with the entry of the soloist and
there is no independent C section. (5) The R1 B theme moves
through various non-tonic keys before returning to the tonic for
a C section. See Julian Horton, 'Beethoven's Error? The
Modulating Ritornello and the Type-5 Sonata in the Post-Classical
Piano Concerto', *Music Analysis* 40/3 (2021): 353–412.

31. On the division of the development section into pre-core, core and
retransition (RT), see William E. Caplin, *Analyzing Classical Form:
An Approach for the Classroom* (New York: Oxford University
Press, 2013), 421–3.

32. Simon P. Keefe, 'Dramatic Dialogue in Mozart's Viennese Piano
Concertos: A Study of Competition and Cooperation in Three First
Movements', *Musical Quarterly* 83/2 (1999): 169–204 and at
greater length, *Mozart's Piano Concertos: Dramatic Dialogue in
the Age of Enlightenment* (Woodbridge: Boydell, 2001).

33. Rink, *Chopin: The Piano Concertos*, 3.

34. Keefe, 'Dramatic Dialogue', 197.
35. On which subject see Dana Gooley, 'The Battle against Instrumental Virtuosity in the Early Nineteenth Century', in Christopher H. Gibbs and Dana Gooley, eds., *Franz Liszt and His World* (Princeton, NJ: Princeton University Press, 2006), 75–111.

2

THE GENESIS OF SCHUMANN'S PIANO CONCERTO

Early Efforts

Schumann's path to the piano concerto was complex and protracted. It encompassed not only abortive compositional attempts, which extend back more than a decade before the completion of the *Phantasie* into the composer's youth, but also variegated critical engagement with the concerti of his time, which produced documentary evidence of an evolving relationship with the genre that is essential for an understanding of both Op. 54's genesis and its compositional strategies.

Schumann's earliest attempt to write a piano concerto dates from 1827, when the seventeen-year-old composer, then still resident in Zwickau, noted in his *Projektenbuch* that he was developing ideas for a Concerto in E minor. According to Schumann's diaries, a Concerto in E flat major was also planned the following year, for which no materials endure; and in the same year he sketched eight bars of a Concerto in C minor, which advanced no further.[1] Considerably more progress was made with a Concerto in F major that preoccupied Schumann in 1830–1. Extensive sketches for this piece can be found in the so-called First Sketchbook. As Claudia Macdonald has shown, they amount to a first movement that is complete apart from the latter stages of R1 and fragments of a finale, which, as Macdonald summarises, consist of 'the first thematic area . . . with two revisions . . . a sketch for the second thematic area . . . also with two revisions . . . and a table showing two motives from [the first theme] and one from [the second theme]'.[2]

The first-movement sketches reveal Schumann engaging closely with recent virtuoso exemplars, particularly Hummel's

Op. 85, Ries' Op. 55, Kalkbrenner's Op. 61 and Herz's Op. 34, a debt evident not only in material similarities but also in explicit formal modelling. This is schematically apparent in the tables that Schumann included in the sketches, which compare aspects of the movement with the corresponding features of paradigmatic compositions, especially Herz's Op. 34 and Ries' Op. 55. The table found on p. 46 of the First Sketchbook, for instance, transcribed by Macdonald and reproduced in Table 2.1, describes the movement's complete form and makes a running comparison with Herz, laying out the principal formal sections in the left-hand column and noting their length in bars in the middle column and the lengths of the corresponding passages in Herz's Op. 34 on the right.[3] The table shows that Schumann worked with a clear overall sense of concerto first-movement form drawn from virtuoso

Table 2.1 *Schumann, Concerto in F major, tabulation of form including comparisons with Herz's Op. 34, transcribed in Macdonald (1986, 89)*

Line	Solo	Section			Herz	
1	1stes Solo	Einleitung mit Thema. 1 & 2.	32		Herz 29.	
2		Einleitg. Ins zweite Thema	31	119.	26	120
3		3 Thema mit Nachspiel	21	128.	21.	
4		Schlussperiode	~~35~~ 42		44.	
5	Tutti					128
6		Thema. 1.	11		39. 39.	69 122
7	2tes Solo	Thema 2. verarb.	56			319
8		Thema 1.	8	66		
9		Tutti	4.	122		
10	3tes Solo	Thema. 2.	8.	49.	23.	89
11		Einleitung ins 3te Thema	8.		15	248
12		3 Thema mit Nachsp.	21.	264	19	
13		Schlussperiode	~~46~~ 62.		32	

examples, and that he was keen to establish both the proportions of his own composition and how they related to Herz's practice. At significant formal junctures, Schumann also calculates the length of larger formal units, summing Herz's S1 to 120 bars in comparison with the 128 bars of S1 in his own movement.

In general, the style of Schumann's material is in keeping with that of his exemplars.[4] As Example 2.1 shows, his S1 begins with an expansive preface and cantabile episode, the former albeit favouring rapid arpeggiated flourishes over the chordal or octave incipits examined in Chapter 1. The transition is demarcated conventionally with a tonic perfect authentic cadence (PAC), and Schumann also maintains virtuoso precedent by allocating different first themes to R1 and S1. Further comparison is, however, conjectural because, even in its most substantial form, the draft of R1 discontinues before it consolidates the second theme. Schumann gets as far as a putative tonic half-close medial caesura (MC) at bar 21 but digresses to A flat major in bar 25 for an idea, quoted in Example 2.2, which begins with a variant of the A theme's head motive but quickly takes on a different character. This material is quite different from S1's B theme, as Example 2.2 also makes clear; but there is no way to establish whether Schumann intended to introduce S1 B later in R1.

For the most part, Schumann's display episodes cleave stylistically to virtuoso precedent. One striking departure appears with the entry of S1 C, quoted in Example 2.3. The B theme does not close with the expected PAC in V but rather dissipates with a plain octave interjection in the cellos and horns, which insinuates an arrival on C as the local tonic without cadential confirmation. The display episode then begins over V/V following a caesura, and no structural cadence subsequently occurs until R2 arrives at bar 135 of the S1 Sketch, some fifty-seven bars later. In sonata theory's terms, S1 effectively has no essential expositional closure (EEC); that is, no cadence rounding off the second theme and ushering in the closing section. Instead, the whole of the second theme and the display episode occupy one large span of music in advance of a cadence. To adopt sonata theory's terminology, bars 78–134 are a species of $C^{PRE-EEC}$, meaning a display episode closing section that produces the dominant structural cadence rather than following it. Since this

Example 2.1 Schumann, F major Concerto, S1 A and start of TR. Reproduced from Macdonald (1986).

music is revisited, with minor adaptations, in the tonic at the recapitulation's corresponding point, the same issue recurs there as well: the essential structural closure (ESC) is located only four bars from the movement's end, as the recapitulation's $C^{PRE-ESC}$ finds a structural V–I.

Example 2.1 (cont.)

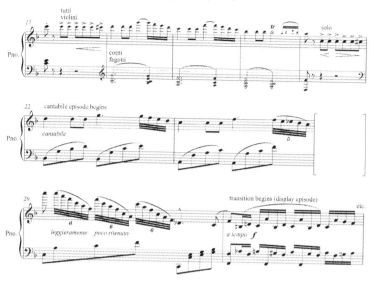

The development is altogether more conventional. It begins with a bravura pre-core redolent of the S1 preface, which ultimately produces a PAC in A flat major articulating the start of the development's core. From this point, Schumann makes very little effort to vary or develop expositional material in any meaningful way; nor is there any obvious reference to the themes of R1 or S1. Instead, he focuses on spinning out *brillante* passagework for some fifty-two bars, until the home dominant has been secured and S1 A returns in the tonic following a brief liquidation of the display texture *senza misura*.

The distance between the generic concepts evidenced in the F major Concerto and in Op. 54 is considerable. The Concerto of 1830–1 is essentially a pedagogical exercise which reveals Schumann absorbing the prevalent concerted style of the time and perhaps staking out his own claims as a fledgling virtuoso. Notwithstanding localised innovations, the F major Concerto makes no significant statement about the genre and signals no aspiration to move beyond paradigms inherited from the first

Example 2.2 Schumann, F major Concerto, sketch for R1 and S1 B. Adapted from Macdonald (1986).

three decades of the nineteenth century. The foundations of Op. 54's far more radical stance were laid over the next decade, as Schumann took stock of new compositions, consolidated his

Example 2.3 Schumann, F major Concerto, end of S1 B and start of C display episode. Adapted from Macdonald (1986).

music-historical thinking and surveyed the genre's expanding horizons and accompanying challenges.

Robert Schumann and Clara Wieck's Piano Concerto Op. 7

The next factor that influenced Schumann's perception of the genre during this time was his involvement in Clara Wieck's Piano Concerto, composed between 1832 and 1835 and published as her Op. 7 in 1837. According to Nancy Reich, Schumann first encountered his future wife, then aged nine, in March 1828 at the Leipzig home of the physician Ernst August Carus, accompanied by her father Friedrich, who would become Schumann's teacher.[5] Schumann lodged with the Wiecks between 1830 and 1831, and from this time developed an increasingly close artistic and personal friendship with Clara, which developed into a fully fledged relationship in 1835, shortly after her sixteenth birthday.[6]

Schumann had at least a partial hand in Op. 7's orchestration. Clara composed the Finale first, most likely as a standalone concert piece, reporting its completion in her diary in autumn of 1833 and noting that 'Schumann now wants to orchestrate it, so that I can play it in my concert'.[7] In September 1835, however, Wieck wrote to Schumann, announcing that the whole concerto was finished and that she had begun work on its orchestration.[8] It received its premiere at the Leipzig Gewandhaus on 9 November 1835, with Clara as soloist and Mendelssohn conducting, and was reviewed in the *Neue Zeitschrift für Musik*. The authorship of the review is unclear. Macdonald accredits it to Robert, an attribution supported by its references to his artistic alter-egos Florestan and Eusebius, but it is signed 'Serpentin', a pseudonym normally used when Schumann delegated work to other authors, most often Carl Banck.[9] The reviewer praised the work's material in floral metaphors, recalling that 'passionate white roses and pearly lily cups leaned over, orange blossoms and myrtle nodded above, and in between, alders and weeping willows cast their melancholy shadows'. He viewed its form less favourably, likening its progress to 'boats [*Kähne*] floating boldly above the waves' which lacked 'a master's grip at the helm [*ein Meistergriff am Steuer*]' and 'a tautened sail [*ein straff gezogenes Segel*]' that might have steered them safely to harbour.[10]

Schumann's compositional debt to Wieck's Op. 7 in Op. 54 has been sketched by John Daverio:

Even Clara may have provided an important but unacknowledged model for [Op. 54]. Her own A minor Concerto Op. 7, completed between 1832 and 1835 under the watchful eyes of her father and her future husband, contains many features that resonate with Schumann's later composition: the overall A minor tonic; the extended episode in A flat in the first movement (comparable to the central Andante, also in A flat, in the *Phantasie*); the monomotivicism of the outer movements; the punctuating melodic descent (D-C-B-A) of the finale's coda (a gesture taken up in Schumann's march-coda). None of these elements counts for much in isolation, but taken together they strengthen the case for viewing Clara's concerto as a source of inspiration for her husband's.[11]

Daverio here overstates some connections and understates others. As we will see, neither of Op. 54's outer movements is, strictly speaking, monomotivic, and neither are the outer movements of Wieck's Op. 7; rather, both concerti treat the head motive of their first movement's main theme cyclically. In Wieck's case, the Finale's first theme is a topical transformation of the first movement's first theme: a march becomes a polonaise but the theme's melodic contour remains unchanged, as Example 2.4 shows.[12] In Op. 54, the first movement's head motive returns in the transition

Example 2.4 Wieck, Op. 7, comparison of first-movement and Finale first themes.

between slow movement and Finale, and consequently serves more as a reminiscence than as a transformation.

Although 'Serpentin' prized Op. 7's content over its form, Schumann's Op. 54 seems to take more from Op. 7's form than from its content. The *Phantasie* of 1841, which would eventually become Op. 54's first movement, explores an ambition, expressed in Schumann's critical writings, to fold the genre's movement types into a single movement; it thereby prefigures the experiments with conflating movement form and movement cycle into a 'two-dimensional' sonata form, which would develop more fully in Liszt's works of the 1850s. One key element of this is the presence of an A flat *andante espressivo* episode at the start of Op. 54's development section, which Macdonald, following August Gerstmeier, has interpreted as an interpolated slow movement.[13] Daverio relates this to 'the extended episode in A flat in the first movement' of Wieck's Concerto; yet her strategy is more radical than he suggests because the A flat episode is not part of the first movement but is a slow movement in its own right. Wieck's first movement is, furthermore, incomplete, consisting of an exposition, which comprises an orchestral introduction, bravura solo entry, first theme, transition, second theme, lengthy display episode closing section and framing tutti, which closes the exposition in the dominant major, having previously insinuated F as the secondary key at the second theme's closing cadence. The movement, however, gets no further than this; instead, there is a modulating transition into the slow movement.[14]

The parallel with Schumann's *Phantasie* is consequently closer than Daverio avers because the corresponding music in Op. 7 occupies the same formal span as well as following the same tonal trajectory: in both cases, a sonata exposition beginning in A minor elides with an A flat slow movement. To be sure, Schumann diverges from Wieck in crucial respects. The tonal scheme of his exposition is less complex, travelling from A minor to C major with reasonable efficiency, whereas Wieck progresses from A minor to E major via C, F and A flat. More obviously, Schumann does not experiment with incomplete forms but houses the exposition and *andante espressivo* within an overarching sonata form. In his critical writings, Schumann viewed the practice of leaving movements formally incomplete with considerable suspicion, conveying his reservations about Clara's adoption of it in private communication.[15] In this respect, Wieck's design has more in common with Moscheles' *Concerto fantastique* Op. 90 of 1833, a work she certainly knew, the first movement of which also elides with the slow movement following a tutti rounding the exposition and a transitory solo entry.

Nevertheless, Wieck's Op. 7 is demonstrably closer to the approach Schumann eventually takes in Op. 54 than anything in his F major Concerto. Opus 7's formal strategies are moreover in dialogue with a kind of concerted composition, instantiated by Moscheles' Op. 90, Mendelssohn's two mature concerti and Weber's *Konzertstück* in F minor, which favours a more radical rethinking of classical form than the model offered by Herz's Op. 34. Wieck, in sum, asked questions of the genre which became central to Schumann's thinking in Op. 54.

Critical Writings, 1835–40

Although Schumann's own compositional interest in the piano concerto lay dormant between 1831 and 1839, he remained highly engaged with other composers' concerti, exemplified above all in his lively critical writings for the *Neue Zeitschrift für Musik*, which survey the field with a sharp eye and sketch a generic vision that Op. 54 ultimately realises. Schumann reviewed some twenty-five works in this period, ranging from compositions that linger in the canon (by Mendelssohn, Chopin and Weber) or at least on its periphery (by Hummel, Field, Moscheles, Bennett, Herz, Ries, Hiller, Taubert and Thalberg) to music that has since disappeared without trace (by Lasekk, Döhler, Hartknoch, Schörnstein and Stamaty). Crucially, these reviews not only document Schumann's critical opinions but also afford insights into the evolution of his thinking about concerted composition. As Macdonald observes:

> often enough Schumann merges his plans as a composer with his work as a critic. While ostensibly commenting, suggesting and dispensing advice to others, he is actually fashioning ideas for his own use. He is, as it were, working out specifics of a new form and style that were to emerge later in a composition of his own, namely, the *Phantasie* [of 1841].[16]

Schumann's foundational ideas are succinctly expressed in the article 'Das Clavier-Concert' of January 1839, in which he sets out an agenda that closely anticipates the *Phantasie*'s technique. 'Das Clavier-Concert' sketches a history of keyboard composition from Bach and Handel onward, which for Schumann is defined by keyboard instruments' gradual separation from the orchestra. The essential problem confronting early nineteenth-century com-posers is the piano's increasing self-containment as an instrument that could meet composers' material and expressive needs without orchestral intervention. As he narrates:

> With the ever-progressing mechanics of piano-playing, which took a bold upswing with Beethoven's compositions, the instrument grew in range and significance, and if it comes to the point, (as I believe), at which a pedal is applied to it, as on the organ, then new prospects open up for the composer and, freeing himself more and more from the supporting orchestra, he will then know how to move even more richly, more fully voiced and more independently.[17]

This, for Schumann, accounts for the paucity of recent piano concerti: 'in defiance of the symphony [*Der Symphonie zum Trotz*], modern piano playing wants to prevail only through its own, fine means, and this may be the reason why so few piano concertos have been produced recently, and few original compos-itions with accompaniment at all'.[18] Reference to the symphony here is significant. Schumann in effect installs keyboard compos-ition as a constitutive alternative to the symphony, or as a kind of symphonic composition having no need of the orchestra: as pianist-composers explored the instrument's capabilities on its own terms, so they followed an independent path in pursuit of a mode of composition that is not simply an annex of symphonism. As Juan Martin Koch explains: 'Schumann justified the supposed decline in piano concerto production with the striving of the piano virtuosi for independence, the formulation "in defiance of the symphony" refers to the generally prevailing symphonic style, which now extends to solo piano music.'[19]

Schumann levelled his sternest criticisms at pianist-composers whose concerti exacerbated rather than ameliorated the piano–orchestra dualism. The most oft-quoted instance appears in his 1836 review of Friedrich Kalkbrenner's Concerto No. 4, a work that failed, for Schumann, because it strayed, in pursuit of Romantic novelty, from the example Kalkbrenner had established in his earlier concerti, which replicated the 'old' forms Schumann discovered in works by Hummel, Field and Herz. The result was 'an aesthetic misfortune' (*ein ästhetisches Unglück*), arising from the fact that Kalkbrenner 'had no talent for romantic impudence' (*er hat kein Talent zur romantischen Frechheit*). Kalkbrenner's Romantic turn remained indebted to the older, virtuoso model of concerto first-movement form, but the self-sufficiency of his piano writing further delineated the solo passages and the orchestral tuttis, between which there was no evident interaction. Thus, Schumann reprimanded 'composers of concert-concerti' who 'have finished their solos and have them ready before the tuttis', hypothesising that Kalkbrenner had 'invented and inserted' his orchestral ritornelli after the fact. This produced a form that articulates the historical separation of piano and orchestra and threatens formal disjunction; as Schumann asks rhetorically: 'Isn't it altogether more difficult to pick up a broken thread (particularly musical ones, which are such that each knot can be figured out with critical antennae) than to quietly move away from it?'[20]

These criticisms are underpinned by a strain of idealism which is both aesthetic and, in an important sense, cultural-political. Virtuosi who privileged the piano over the orchestra very often did so to the ends of self-aggrandisement and self-advancement.

Schumann was especially suspicious of the varieties of Parisian virtuosity, in which aesthetic narcissism had obvious pecuniary motivations.[21] In his review of Herz's Concerto No. 2, published in 1836, Schumann openly accused the composer of superficiality in the service of financial gain, asking, 'What more does he wish than to amuse – and grow rich?'[22] Persistently counterpointing Herz's opportunism and Beethoven's artistic integrity, Schumann ends by positing the latter as an antidote to the former: 'Herz's Second Concerto is in C minor, and is recommended to those who liked the first. Should it by chance be placed in a programme also containing a certain Symphony in C minor [i.e., Beethoven's Fifth], one prays that the symphony will follow the concerto.'[23] This critique exemplifies a broader Francophobia, which is especially marked in Schumann's response to Meyerbeer's *Les Huguenots*. Observing with exasperation that 'Meyerbeer's success in our musically healthy Germany is enough to make one question one's own sanity', he denounced *Les Huguenots* as an affront to Germany's religious heritage, motivated purely by the pursuit of money and fame: 'I am not a moralist, but a good Protestant is outraged to see their most valued song [the Lutheran chorale *Ein feste Burg*] shouted out from the stage, outraged to see the bloodiest drama of religious history reduced to the farce of a funfair simply to earn money and notoriety.'[24]

In 'Das Clavier-Concert', Schumann set out a vision for the genre which hitches its fortunes to the resolution of the piano-orchestral dichotomy, and which, necessarily, would also entail a repudiation of Parisian opportunism at the hands of German idealism. The piano concerto awaits a composer, so Schumann tells us, who will arrest the genre's decline by deconstructing the mutually exclusive self-sufficiency of the piano and orchestra, exploring fresh possibilities for their combination:

One would certainly have to call it a loss, were the piano concerto with orchestra to fall completely out of use; on the other hand, we can hardly contradict the pianists, when they say 'we have no need of external aids [*andere Beihülfe*]; our instrument works perfectly by itself'. And so we must confidently await the genius who shows us in a brilliant new way how the orchestra can be combined with the piano, how the soloist can unfold the richness of his instrument and his art, while the orchestra does more than merely spectate and weaves its manifold characters into the scene.[25]

The challenge Schumann poses here has textural, material and formal dimensions. The core of the textural dilemma faced in combining piano and orchestra is the question of how two self-sufficient media can be merged to produce something that is more than the sum of its parts. This is also a material challenge because a putative solution to the textural question resides in the perception that soloist and orchestra should have joint responsibility for thematic content and should therefore collaborate in its presentation, elaboration and development. The challenge is formal because the type 5 sonata that virtuoso composers inherited from the late eighteenth century encourages a division of orchestral and solo labour that inhibits their integration, a trap into which Kalkbrenner conspicuously fell. Consequently, any solution to the historical question of the divergence of piano and orchestra is also an exploration of new concerted forms.

Schumann's critical writings review several works, referred to by Macdonald as the 'new forms', which open up fresh formal possibilities.[26] One idea, which we have already encountered in Clara Wieck's Concerto, is to elide the genre's movement cycle. Schumann's critical reception of this innovation varied depending on whether or not the elided movements are formally complete. In an 1836 review of Carl Lasekk's B minor Concertino, Schumann reacted unsympathetically, noting that 'dilettante' composers of concertinos 'which are made up of various movements in differing tempos that merge into one another' risked committing 'an aesthetic mishap [*ein ästhetisches Malheur*]' if they failed to secure the individual movements' formal integrity in a fully fledged concerto.[27] Works by Mendelssohn and Taubert exhibiting inter-movement continuity sidestepped this risk because their elided movements are complete in themselves. Reviewing Mendelssohn's Concerto No. 1, Op. 25, Schumann perceived no formal omissions, and only noted that 'it should never occur to me to write a concerto in three contiguous movements [*drei aneinander geschlossenen Sätzen*]'; he regarded

Taubert's Concerto Op. 18, which is closely modelled on
Mendelssohn's Op. 25, as an extension of the same practice.
On the other hand, Moscheles' *Concerto fantastique* Op. 90,
like Wieck's Op. 7, omits formal regions in three of its four
elided movements, thereby straying into dangerous territory
and compelling Schumann to observe that 'Even though it
doesn't seem impossible to make a satisfactory whole of it, the
aesthetic danger is simply too great, measured against what can
be achieved.'[28]

If Schumann's reception of these innovations seems cautious,
his preferred solution, outlined in the review of Moscheles' Op.
90, is far more radical. There is, he suggests,

> a lack of smaller concert pieces in which the virtuoso could unfold the Allegro-
> Adagio-Rondo sequence in a single movement. One should think of a genre
> consisting of a one-movement composition in moderate tempo [*einem größern
> Satz in einem mässigen Tempo*], in which the preparatory part [*der vorbereitende
> Theil*] would take the place of the first allegro, the cantabile section [*die
> Gesangstelle*] that of the adagio, and a brilliant conclusion that of the rondo.[29]

Schumann, in other words, proposes a two-dimensional sonata
form in which the large-scale formal subdivisions have the character of a concerto's individual movements. This idea addresses
the dualism of piano and orchestra and the 'aesthetic hazards'
courted by Moscheles' and Wieck's incomplete forms at the
same time. Schumann's rejection of the older type 5 first-movement form in favour of what is in effect a symphonic sonata (the
standard 'type 3' sonata in Hepokoski and Darcy's terms) removes
the ritornello–solo division of labour, and thereby forces the
permanent formal cohabitation of soloist and orchestra, who
must collaborate in the presentation and development of material.
And because the sequence of movements now sits within an
overarching sonata form, the threat of formal incoherence detected
in the use of incomplete forms disappears, since all implied movement types contribute to a form which is complete in itself. With
this concept, Schumann cleared the ground for renewed compositional efforts, of which the *Phantasie* of 1841 and the Concerto of
1845 are the ultimate fruit.

The Concerto of 1839

Schumann made one further attempt at concerto composition before conceiving the *Phantasie* in 1841.[30] Between October 1838 and April 1839, he was resident in Vienna where he hoped to find a replacement publisher for the *Neue Zeitschrift für Musik*, during which time he worked intensively on a Concerto in D minor intended for Clara, reference to which is made in a letter to her dated 9 January 1839:

> My dearest Clara, my tardiness in answering your letter from Nüremberg, which I received on Wednesday, is to be blamed solely on the beautiful concerto in D minor (with accompaniment) which my sweetheart is drawing from me, and from which I could not tear myself away yesterday or the day before .... The first movement is finished, and the instrumentation is coming along very well; it is neither difficult to play, nor to understand.[31]

By 26 January, however, Schumann's momentum had faltered, as further correspondence to Clara of that date attests:

> I spent all of last week composing, but am dissatisfied with my ideas, and feel devoid of sweet melancholy. I already told you about the concerto; it is a cross between a symphony, a concerto and a grand sonata. It is clear that I cannot write a concerto for the virtuoso; I must think of something else. Nonetheless, I should be finished within eight days.[32]

In the end, Schumann only made meaningful progress on the first movement, the sketches and drafts for which are now housed in Bonn University Library. In 1986, a reconstruction and completion were attempted by the Belgian pianist Jozef De Beenhouwer, which was subsequently edited by Joachim Draheim and published, in 1988, by Breitkopf and Härtel under the title *Konzertsatz*. Any analytical observations on the movement must remain tentative, given Draheim's insistence that the edition should be understood as 'a carefully pondered contribution towards a reconstruction of this work' rather than a 'definitive version'. For example, it includes a cadenza of some sixty-three bars composed by De Beenhouwer, which, as Draheim explains, 'is oriented on Schumann's original cadenza in the first movement of the Piano Concerto in A minor, Op. 54', but is not based on any surviving material at this point in the manuscript.[33]

Nevertheless, there is enough evidence to reveal a crucial shift in Schumann's conception of the genre, which adds weight to his conviction that the work 'is a cross between a symphony, a concerto and a grand sonata' and points to the close relationship between its conception and the agenda laid out in 'Das Clavier-Concert'.[34] Above all, the movement does away with the type 5 sonata form with which Schumann engaged in the F major Concerto in 1831, replacing it with a variant of the type 3 model common to symphonies, overtures and sonatas and thereby prefiguring the *Phantasie* (the form is summarised in Table 2.2). There are no ritornelli and very few orchestral tuttis. The movement aligns most closely with a variant of sonata form that Steven Vande Moortele has shown to be widely employed in concert overtures of the period, in which the exposition's closing section merges with the development without a discernible break.[35] Soloist and orchestra collaborate in the presentation of a terse periodic sixteen-bar theme (Example 2.5), preceded by a five-bar slow introduction and followed immediately by a transition.

The *Konzertsatz* shuns virtuosity to a significant extent, favouring piano writing that owes more to the athematic figuration of the Baroque keyboard prelude than to the style of the virtuoso concerto. As Macdonald points out, Schumann's approach may betray evidence of his encounter with J. S. Bach's Triple Concerto in D minor, BWV 1063, which he heard in Leipzig in 1835, as well as Mendelssohn's Piano Concerto No. 2, Op. 40, also in D minor, reviewed in the article 'Das Clavier-Concert', in which Schumann singled out Bach's influence, observing that it 'is here and there discernible in the harmonic progressions'.[36] Baroque harmonic and textural proclivities are notably apparent in the *Konzertsatz*'s expositional closing section and development, which are fused without demarcation. This entire passage, spanning from bars 70–216, is constructed almost exclusively from sequential treatment of the motive quoted in Example 2.6, which first appears in the transition. The extract from the closing section cited in Example 2.7 is typical: the orchestra supplies the framework of a model progression in bars 80–3, which is sequenced down a step in 84–7 and fragmented through a descending cycle of fifths in 88–96. The soloist maintains the transition motive throughout. In a

Table 2.2 *Schumann, Konzertsatz in D minor, form*

Bars:	1	6	22	46	70	208	216	280	296	311
Form:	intro.	exposition ⇒ development						recapitulation?		coda
		A	TR	B	C	RT	[cadenza]	B	A	
Key:	i		i→	III	III→	V/i			i	

Example 2.5 Schumann, *Konzertsatz*, first theme.

Example 2.6 Schumann, *Konzertsatz*, start of transition.

technique foreshadowing the *Phantasie*, Schumann inverts the virtuoso relationship between display and theme: rather than treating display as an end in itself, to which motivic material contributes, the severe restriction of the soloist to a single motive renders display an incidental biproduct of motivic repetition, producing a texture more redolent of Baroque *Fortspinnung* than virtuoso extroversion.

The *Konzertsatz* also anticipates the *Phantasie*'s tendency towards harmonic evasion. The second theme, for instance, quoted in Example 2.8, prolongs the relative major obliquely rather than unequivocally and closes with a cadence, the resolution of which is undercut by multiple suspensions. These ambiguities later

Example 2.7 Schumann, *Konzertsatz*, bars 80–96.

impact the piece's form. *Pace* Draheim's explanation, De Beenhouwer's reconstruction positions the cadenza over the dominant before any discernible recapitulation has occurred, suggesting that he has located it at the point of retransition, whereas in Op. 54

Example 2.8 Schumann, *Konzertsatz*, start of B theme and start of closing section.

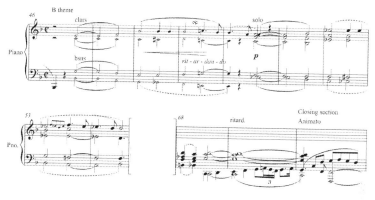

the cadenza falls between the recapitulation and the coda.[37] De Beenhouwer's cadenza is followed by a highly compressed reprise of the second and first themes in reverse order. The second theme's return concomitantly sustains its harmonic equivocation, delaying the resolution of the retransition's dominant until the first-theme return at bar 296, which is coordinated with a definitive tonic arrival. Although the *Konzertsatz* does not experiment with two-dimensional form and consequently does not fully realise the aspirations Schumann expressed in his critical writings, it takes a significant step towards that goal.

The *Phantasie* of 1841 and the Concerto of 1845

Finally, in 1841, Schumann was able to pursue his ambitions for a new kind of piano concerto to completion. The composition of the *Phantasie* is closely bound up with the three other major projects that define what Daverio calls Schumann's 'symphonic year': the Symphony No. 1; the work that would eventually become the Symphony No. 4; and the Overture, Scherzo and Finale (the '*Symphonette*', as Schumann described it).[38] The *Phantasie*'s progress is recorded in the Schumanns' marriage diary (*Ehetagebuch*) and household diary (*Haushaltbuch*). Robert noted the work's inception in the household diary on 3 May

1841, and this is confirmed by Clara's entry on the following day.[39] Thereafter, Schumann made rapid progress. In an entry in the marriage diary dated 10–22 May, he describes the *Phantasie* as 'fully orchestrated [*fertig instrumentirt*]', in tandem with work on the Overture, Scherzo and Finale.[40] The diary entry breaks down the stages of composition, announcing the music's completion on 14 May and work on its orchestration between 15 and 20 May.[41] By 12 August, the manuscript had been dispatched to Schumann's copyist; and on the following day, the *Phantasie* was included in a trial rehearsal, together with the Symphony No. 1, at the Leipzig Gewandhaus, with Clara at the piano and Ferdinand David conducting.

Schumann's efforts to publish the work, however, proved as protracted as its composition was swift. Wolfgang Boetticher and Mahn-Hee Kang cite an unsuccessful approach to Friedrich Kistner as his first known attempt at publication; a letter of 5 November 1842 to Schuberth in Hamburg also yielded nothing; and letters to Whistling, Hoffman and Peters in 1843 proved similarly futile.[42] Eventually, in December 1843 Schumann wrote to Breitkopf and Härtel, offering them the oratorio *Das Paradies und die Peri*, adding that 'I will be happy to offer you a smaller composition, and I suggest a concert-allegro for piano with orchestral accompaniment.'[43] Breitkopf accepted on the condition that he add a slow movement and Finale, thereby enlarging the *Phantasie* into a fully fledged concerto. Schumann did not, however, resume work until the summer of 1845. Diary entries for June of that year track the Finale's progress, indicating that it was orchestrated between 1 and 12 July. The slow movement followed in quick succession: by 16 July, Schumann could announce in the *Tagebuch* that it was completed. These dates are corroborated by the manuscript: the end of the Finale bears the date 12 June 1845, the first page of the Intermezzo 16 July and the end of the first movement 29 July, indicating that revisions to the *Phantasie* were made in light of the subsequent movements. This compositional history is apostrophised on the manuscript's title page: Schumann announced the work as an 'Allegro quazi Fantasia, Intermezzo and Rondo', beneath which a pencil annotation reads 'Allegro Leipzig 1841. Intermezzo u. Rondo Dresden 1845'.

Reconstructing the process through which Schumann reimagined the *Phantasie* as the first movement of Op. 54, Boetticher concluded that the former was converted into the latter with relatively minimal revision; as he explains, 'the biographical data testifies to the great stability of the *Phantasie*', which transferred into the Concerto 'without the structure meanwhile becoming harmed'.[44] Yet no independent source for the *Phantasie* survives; Boetticher's conclusions are reached purely on the basis of scattered entries in Schumann's *Haushaltbuch* and the marriage diary. The autograph manuscript of Op. 54's first movement displays numerous layers of revision, but whether peeling them back reveals the *Phantasie* in its original conception is hard to determine. The first-movement manuscript differs from that of the Intermezzo and Finale in that the solo piano part is not in Schumann's hand but is a copy, which, according to Bernhard Appel, was prepared by Carl Gottschalk in 1845.[45] It is likely, although not conclusively demonstrable, that this piano part is substantially that of the *Phantasie*, beneath which Schumann added the orchestration; and it may also be the case that the orchestral music subjected to revision in the autograph was carried over from the *Phantasie*. But since no other source survives, the extent of the 'stability' that Boetticher describes is impossible to establish. Appel rightly defines the manuscript as an 'Arbeitspartitur' or 'working score', which constitutes an intermediate stage between the *Phantasie*'s first conception and the first edition.[46]

Revisions are applied to the manuscript in several ways. Often, Schumann simply crossed out music he wanted to replace and overwrote it with the alternative. One of the most striking instances occurs in the first movement's introduction, the two versions of which apparent in the manuscript are compared in Example 2.9. Opus 54 (Example 2.9b) begins with a tutti orchestral hammer blow on the dominant, to which the soloist's initial flourish responds. This is a later addition: the early conception (Example 2.9a) deploys identical solo material, but the orchestra enters simultaneously, supporting the pianist with an E octave, prefaced by the same dotted semitone anacrusis as the piano, pitched a minor ninth below the pianist's soprano E on D sharp. To indicate the change, Schumann drew multiple vertical lines through the original string parts in ink and added the hammer blow

Example 2.9 Schumann, *Phantasie* and Op. 54/i, comparison of introductions.

in place of the initial orchestral rests, which, as Figure 2.1 shows, are scribbled over. Schumann also revised the pianist's part in the emphatic V–i progression ushering in the first theme in bars 3–4: the pianist's chordal doubling of the string parts in Op. 54 is overwritten onto the original music, blacked out with bold pen strokes, which allocated chords to the piano in the same tenor register in which the descending bravura flourish concludes.

The unrevised opening generates a harmonic complexity which is absent in Op. 54. The soloist's progression, analysed in Example 2.10, emphasises chord VI[6], arrived at via an anacrusic augmented

Figure 2.1 Schumann, Op. 54, autograph manuscript, first page of first movement.

triad that functions as a neighbouring-chord prefix. The VI[6] chord is comprehensible in relation to the orchestra's E as itself a neighbouring chord, which sits above a dominant pedal. The orchestra's D sharp prefix has no harmonic function at all: it is not part of the soloist's augmented triad and must be understood purely melodically, as a chromatic lower neighbour note to V. This chromatic tangle clarifies at the introduction's end, where the first theme is ushered in via a V $^6_4$ –V[7]–i progression. As Example 2.10 explains, the soloist's material really serves altogether to prolong $\hat{6}$, which it transfers down two octaves from the c[3] to the c[1] registers before resolving as a neighbour to $\hat{5}$. The sense of F as a prolonged neighbour to E is also present in Op. 54, but more by implication because the orchestra's overall prolongation of the dominant is implicit rather than explicit: it is insinuated by the hammer blow rather than asserted against the soloist's VI chord.

In three places, Schumann rejected the *Phantasie*'s piano part wholesale. The first notable change affects the way in which the exposition ends. Schumann's first idea is preserved in the

Example 2.10 Schumann, *Phantasie*, introduction, harmonic and voice-leading analysis.

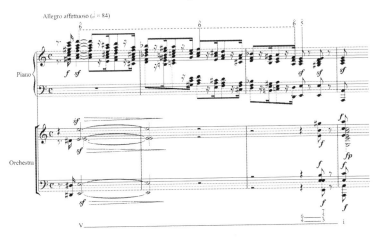

manuscript as an eight-bar transition in the solo part, written in the copyist's hand. Kang concludes that this was conceived for the pianist alone, but it is also possible that it was designed to accompany a shorter version of the orchestral tutti, which eventually occupied this space but was never added below the solo part. The piano figuration here is comparable to that supporting the corresponding passage in the recapitulation (bars 385–8).[47] As Example 2.11 explains, it corresponds harmonically to the first four bars of the tutti in its final version (bars 134–7 in Op. 54), after which Schumann composes a mode switch from C major to C minor, which in Op. 54 arrives fifteen bars later in preparation for the modulation to A flat with the entry of the *andante espressivo* at bar 156. This passage is crossed out in pencil, and a new section, entirely in Schumann's hand, is inserted, introducing the pianist's octave ascent with which the exposition closes in bars 132–3 and the tutti familiar from Op. 54. Schumann duly amended the page numbers: every odd number thereafter is crossed out and the correct number is added by Schumann in pencil.

The second and most substantial revision is made in the development's core starting at bar 205, the entire piano part of which

Example 2.11 Schumann, *Phantasie*, bars 133–41, first version of piano part in manuscript, with final-version tutti material overlaid.

was recomposed. This significant change is not evidenced in the manuscript, a fact which leads Boetticher to conclude that the revision in Schumann's hand is lost.[48] Example 2.12 gives a flavour of the modifications by comparing bars 205–10 in the autograph and in the first edition. In the autograph (Example 2.12a), the first flute carries a variant of the first theme, sometimes enhanced by the violins; the soloist contributes figuration, as the passage's textural interior. In the final version (Example 2.12b), the flute's line is doubled by the pianist, whose figuration is now

Example 2.12 Schumann, *Phantasie* and Op. 54/i, comparison of bars 205–10.

shared between left and right hands. The revision foregrounds thematic action by additionally emphasising the theme, and by making soloist and orchestra joint participants in its presentation.

Example 2.13 Schumann, *Phantasie*, original ending of cadenza.

This change of emphasis is applied all the way from bar 205 to the start of the recapitulation, with a concomitant increase in textural density and the piano part's level of difficulty.

The final wholesale revision appears at the end of the cadenza. Schumann's earlier thoughts are shown in Example 2.13. In bar 446, the music arrives on a cadential $^6_4$ chord, which is elaborated for four bars with figuration growing out of the previous bar's septuplets. The cadenza then concludes with an abrupt two-bar dominant ninth in which the strings also participate, and the soloist underpins the coda, which originally had the tempo designation *quasi presto*, with rolled semiquaver figuration from its inception. The revision, inserted into the manuscript on an additional strip of paper and corresponding to bars 446–61 in the first movement of Op. 54, doubles the length of this passage, capitalising on the potential of the music in bars 442–5 to generate sequences and thereby reaching F major in bars 452–4.

Schumann then returns to the motive with which the cadenza begins, converting F into an augmented sixth chord, which duly resolves to V in bar 456. The marked dominant ninth and its associated descending piano arpeggiation in the original are replaced by a double trill on the dominant, which now persists into the coda (Schumann strikes out the first three and a half bars of the accompaniment and overwrites them with the continuing trill). This revision has a structural impact on the cadenza: the new bars'

Example 2.14 Schumann, *Phantasie* and Op. 54/i, comparison of bars 67–70.

progression through F alludes back to the German augmented sixth chord with which the cadenza begins in bar 398, creating a structural frame on VI, which the original version lacks. The insertion is not in Schumann's hand and is likely the work of the same copyist who prepared the solo part in the manuscript. Boetticher therefore argues that this revision was made at a relatively early stage, although Appel's ascription of the piano part's copy to Gottschalk in 1845 challenges this chronology.[49]

Schumann made numerous further small adjustments to the solo part, but many of the more striking further revisions apply to the orchestration. In several places, Schumann streamlined the solo wind parts; Example 2.14, for instance, compares bars 67–70, which are one candidate for the presentation of the second theme. The clarinet's writing was originally notably soloistic: each phrase terminated in an arpeggiated descent which tracks

Example 2.15 Schumann, Op. 54, transition from Intermezzo to Finale, stages of revision.

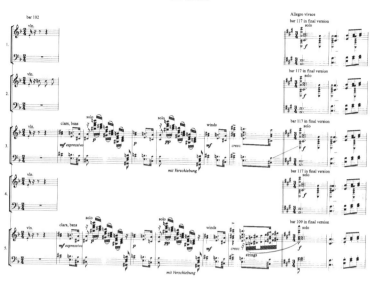

the more rapid descending figuration in the piano's left hand. Schumann's final version is less flamboyant: the clarinet's variant of the first theme is shadowed by the soloist but the descending arpeggiation at the phrase ending is removed. The result is not only a less decorative variant of the theme but also an increased focus on thematic content over display.

According to Stephen Roe, all three movements also show evidence of Clara's interventions, most substantially the Finale, where Robert's hand yields to Clara's for the solo part in bars 529–739, which comprise the recapitulation of the transition, second theme and closing section.[50] The Finale also contains a large number of small-scale revisions to the solo and orchestral parts, but only the transition from the Intermezzo betrays a level of uncertainty comparable to the first movement's larger-scale revisions. The Intermezzo's final page is shown in Figure 2.2. Bernhard Appel has separated the tangle of corrections here into five revisionary levels, summarised in Example 2.15.[51] Schumann's first idea was to

Figure 2.2 Schumann, Op. 54, autograph manuscript, transition between
Intermezzo and Finale.

halt the Intermezzo with the *pianissimo* E in bar 102, reinforced
by the horns, and then proceed directly into what, in the final
version, is bar 9 of the Finale. He then rewrote bar 102, removing
the horn parts and adding a putative violin line, which is then
crossed out. Schumann's third inspiration was to expand the
transition by a further six bars, recovering the first movement's
first theme, interspersed with descending chordal piano interjections and creating the framework of the transition we know
today, but still proceeding into the Finale at its ninth bar. He
then had misgivings about this more complex transition and
reverted to the idea of progressing directly from bar 102 to bar
9 of the Finale. In the end, Schumann returned to the first-
movement recall, adding the now-familiar scalar string flourish
in bar 108 to suture the bridge between the movements, and
inserting an additional page containing the eight-bar in-tempo
introduction adumbrating the Finale's first theme.

Clara was evidently happy with the finished Concerto, com-
menting enthusiastically in her diary: 'What a contrast between

this and Henselt's [Concerto Op. 16, composed in 1844, which Clara performed in Dresden around the same time as Op. 54's first performance]. How rich in invention, how interesting from beginning to end it is; how fresh, and what a beautifully connected whole! I find real pleasure in studying it!'[52] The completed work received a private premiere in Dresden on 4 December, with Clara as soloist and Ferdinand Hiller conducting, and was repeated in Leipzig on 1 January 1846. It was published as a solo piano score and set of parts by Breitkopf and Härtel in 1846; the full-score edition followed posthumously in 1862; and Clara edited a further publication for the complete edition of Schumann's works in 1888. The 1846 first edition signifies more than Op. 54's entry into the world; it completes the gestation of Schumann's concept of the genre, bringing to an end a process of theorising and experimentation spanning nearly two decades.

Notes

1. On Schumann's efforts before 1830, see Man-Hee Kang, 'Robert Schumann's Piano Concerto in A Minor, Op. 54: A Stemmatic Analysis of the Sources' (PhD dissertation: Ohio State University, 1992), 6. On the E minor Concerto, see Georg Eismann, *Robert Schumann: Ein Quellenwerk über sein Leben und Schaffen*, vol. I (Leipzig: Breitkopf und Härtel, 1956), 17. Reference to the E flat Concerto is made in Robert Schumann, *Tagebücher*, vol. I: 1827–38, ed. Georg Eismann (Leipzig: Deutscher Verlag für Musik, 1971), 157.
2. Claudia Macdonald, 'Robert Schumann's F Major Concerto of 1831 As Reconstructed from His First Sketchbook: A History of Its Composition and Study of Its Musical Background' (PhD dissertation: University of Chicago, 1986), 417.
3. Macdonald, 'Robert Schumann's F Major Concerto of 1831 As Reconstructed from His First Sketchbook', 89, and see also *Robert Schumann and the Piano Concerto* (New York: Routledge, 2005), 56.
4. For an analysis of the F major Concerto, see also Stephan D. Lindeman, *Structural Novelty and Tradition in the Early Romantic Piano Concerto* (Stuyvesant: Pendragon Press, 1999), 143–5.
5. On the work's compositional history, see Nancy Reich, *Clara Schumann: The Artist and the Woman* (Ithaca, NY: Cornell University Press, 2013), 227–8.

6. For a narrative of Robert's early relationship with Clara, see Reich, *Clara Schumann*, 45–8.
7. Janina Klassen, '"Schumann will es nun instrumentieren": Das Finale aus Clara Wiecks Klavierkonzert Op. 7 als frühestes Beispiel einer künstlerischen Zusammenarbeit von Robert und Clara Schumann', *Schumann-Studien* 3/4 (1994): 291–9. For a recent consideration of Clara's relationship to the nineteenth-century concerto repertoire, see Joe Davies, 'Clara Schumann and the Nineteenth-Century Piano Concerto', in Joe Davies, ed., *Clara Schumann Studies* (Cambridge: Cambridge University Press, 2021), 95–116.
8. Clara Schumann and Robert Schumann, *Briefwechsel*, vol. 1, *1832–1838*, ed. Eva Weissweiler (Basel: Stroemfeld, 1984), 17.
9. Claudia Macdonald, 'Critical Perception and the Woman Composer: The Early Reception of Piano Concertos by Clara Wieck Schumann and Amy Beach', *Current Musicology* 55 (1993): 24–55, at 27 and also *Robert Schumann and the Piano Concerto*, 161–2. Upon publication, the Concerto was reviewed again in the *Neue Zeitscrhift*, this time by Carl Friedrich Becker; see *Neue Zeitschrift für Musik* 6/14 (17 February 1837): 56–7. Becker's review is considered by Macdonald in *Robert Schumann and the Piano Concerto*, 163. On the authors writing for the *Neue Zeitschrift* at this time, see Annette Vosteen, 'Introduction: *Neue Zeitschrift für Musik* (1834–44)', *Repertoire internationale de la presse musicale* (2001), www.ripm .org/pdf/Introductions/NZM1834-1844introEnglish.pdf.
10. 'Weiße sehnende Rosen und perlende Lilienkelche neigten hinüber, und drüben nickten Orangenblüthen und Myrthen und dazwischen streckten Erlen und Trauerweiden ihre melancholischen Schatten aus'. 'Schwärmbriefe', *Neue Zeitschrift für Musik* 3/46 (1835): 182–3, at 182, translation mine.
11. Daverio, *Robert Schumann*, 237–8.
12. The connection between the movements is pointed out by Benedict Taylor; see 'Clara Wieck's A Minor Piano Concerto: Formal Innovation and the Problem of Parametric Disconnect in Early Romantic Music', *Music Theory and Analysis* 8/11 (2021): 1–28, at 6.
13. Macdonald, 'Mit einer eignen außerordentlichen Composition: The Genesis of Schumann's *Phantasie* in A Minor', *Journal of Musicology* 13/2 (1995): 240–59, at 253–5 and August Gerstmeier, *Robert Schumann: Klavierkonzert A-moll, Op. 54* (Munich: Wilhelm Fink Verlag, 1986), 25.
14. Taylor also reads the first movement as a unitary exposition closed with a tutti in the manner of a classical ritornello 2; see 'Clara Wieck's A Minor Piano Concerto', 13–14.

15. In a letter dated 29 November 1837, Schumann insisted that the first movement 'did not impress me as complete'; see Clara Schumann and Robert Schumann, *Briefwechsel*, vol. 1, 53, cited in Macdonald, 'Mit einer eignen außerordentlichen Composition', 256, n. 45.

16. Macdonald, 'Mit einer eignen außerordentlichen Composition', 247.

17. 'Mit der immer fortschreitenden Mechanik des Clavierspiels, mit dem kühneren Aufschwung, den die Composition durch Beethoven nahm, wuchs auch das Instrument an Umfang und Bedeutung, und kommt es noch dahin, (wie ich glaube), das man an ihm, wie bei der Orgel, ein Pedal in Anwendung bringt, so entstehen dem Componisten neue Aussichten und sich immermehr vom unterstüzenden Orchester losmachend, wird es sich dann noch reicher, vollstimmiger und selbstständiger zu bewegen wissen.' See 'Das Clavier-Concert', *Neue Zeitschrift für Musik* 10/2 (1839): 5–7, at 5, col. 1, translation mine.

18. Ibid., 6, cols. 1–2.

19. '[In the article "Das Clavier-Concert"], in der Schumann den vermeintlichen Rückgang der Klavierkonzertproduktion mit dem Streben der Klaviervirtuosen nach Selbständigkeit begründet, bezieht sich die Formulierung "der Symphonie zum Trotz" auf den allgemein vorherrschenden, nunmehr auf die Soloklaviermusik übergreifenden symphonischen stil.' Koch, *Das Klavierkonzert des 19. Jahrhunderts und die Kategorie des Symphonischen*, 200.

20. 'Und ist's nicht überhaupt schwerer, einen zerrissenen Faden wieder auszunehmen (namentlich musikalische, die so sein daß jeder Knoten herauszufinden mit kritischen Fühlhörnern), als ihn ruhig fortzuziehn?'. 'Pianoforte: Concerte', *Neue Zeitschrift für Musik* 4/27 (1836): 113–14, at 113, col. 1.

21. Schumann's reception of Parisian virtuosity is appraised in Leon Plantinga, *Schumann as Critic* (New Haven, CT: Yale University Press, 1967), 196–207.

22. 'Pianoforte: Concerte', 'Was will er dann als amusiren und nebenbei reich werden?' 'Pianoforte: Concerte', *Neue Zeitschrift für Musik* 4/26 (1836): 110–11, translated as 'Henri Herz: Piano Concerto No. 2' (1836) in Pleasants, ed., *Schumann on Music*, 110–11, at 110.

23. Ibid., 111: 'Das Zweite Concert von Herz geht aus C-Moll und wird denen empfohlen, die das erste lieben. Sollte an einem Concertabende zufällig eine gewisse C-Moll-Symphonie mitgegeben werden, so bittet man selbige nach dem Concert anzusetzen.'

24. 'Ich bin kein Moralist; aber einen guten Protestant empört's, sein theuerstes Lied auf den Bretern abgeschreien zu hören, empört es, das blutigste Drama seiner Religionsgeschichte zu einer Jahrmarktsfarce heruntergezogen zu sehen, Geld und Geschrei damit zu erheben.' Robert Schumann, 'Fragments aus Leipzig',

The Genesis of Schumann's Piano Concerto

Neue Zeitschrift für Musik 7/19 (1837): 73–5, at 73, translated as 'The Huguenots' (1837) in Pleasants, ed., *Schumann on Music*, 137–40, at 138. On Schumann's reception of Meyerbeer, see Plantinga, *Schumann as Critic*, 160–4. Schumann's critique of *Les Huguenots* has been regarded as evidence of anti-Semitism; on which subject see Celia Applegate, *The Necessity of Music: Variations on a German Theme* (Toronto: University of Toronto Press, 2017), 160–4. On attitudes towards the Jewish population in nineteenth-century Saxony, see Simone Lässig, 'Emancipation and Embourgeoisement: The Jews, the State, and the Middle Class in Saxony and Anhalt-Dessau', in James Retallack, ed., *Saxony in German History: Culture, Society, and Politics, 1830–1933* (Ann Arbor: University of Michigan Press, 2000), 99–118.

25. 'Das Clavier-Concert', 6, col. 2.
26. Macdonald, *Robert Schumann and the Piano Concerto*, 135–96.
27. 'Pianoforte: Concerte', *Neue Zeitschrift für Musik* 4/18 (1836): 77. Carl Lasekk was the anagrammatic pseudonym of Baron Karl von Caskel (1797–1874), on whom see Macdonald, *Robert Schumann and the Piano Concerto*, 186–7.
28. 'Scheint es auch nicht unmöglich, in ihr ein wohltuendes Ganzes zu erzeugen, so ist die ästhetische Gefahr zu gross gegen das, was erreicht werden kann', 'Pianoforte: Concerte', *Neue Zeitschrift für Musik* 4/29 (1836): 122–4, at 123, col. 2, translation mine. On the use of incomplete first-movement forms in later-century concerti, see Peter H. Smith, 'Dvořák's Violin Concerto Reconsidered: Joachim's Influence, Bruch's Model and Romantic Innovations in Sonata Practice', *Music Analysis* 41/1 (2022): 3–49.
29. 'Allerdings fehlt es an kleinen Concertstücken, in denen der Virtuose den Allegro-, Adagio-, und Rond-Vortrag zugleich entfalten könnte. Man müßte auf eine Gattung sinnen, die aus einem größern Satz in einem mäßigen Tempo bestände, in dem der vorbereitende Theil die Stelle eines ersten Allegros, die Gesangstelle die des Adagio und ein brillianter Schluß die des Rondos vertreten.' *Neue Zeitschrift für Musik* 4/29 (1836): 122–4, at 123, col. 2, translation mine.
30. On the evidence of its title alone, the *Concert sans orchestra* Op. 14 also merits consideration here. In reality, Op. 14, which began life as a sonata, morphed into the *Concert sans orchestra* in 1836 and was later published as the Piano Sonata No. 3 with one of the scherzi from its original conception restored, does not engage with any concerted principles beyond the fact that its first published version only has three movements, and has no meaningful bearing on the narrative of Op. 54's genesis. Daverio suggests that the title was proposed by the publisher Haslinger 'as a promotional ploy' rather

than a commentary on anything in the work's generic or aesthetic intent. See *Robert Schumann*, 150.

31. *Briefwechsel*, vol. 2, 359.

32. *Briefwechsel*, vol. 2, 367.

33. Joachim Draheim, 'Preface', in Robert Schumann, *Konzertsatz für Klavier und Orchester D-Moll*, reconstructed and completed by Jozef De Beenhouwer, edited by Joachim Draheim (Wiesbaden: Breitkopf und Härtel, 1988), i–xii, at x.

34. For analysis of the *Konzertsatz*, see Macdonald, *Robert Schumann and the Piano Concerto*, 197–22, Kerman, 'The Concertos', 175–6 and Lindeman, *Structural Novelty and Tradition in the Early Romantic Piano Concerto*, 147–52.

35. Steven Vande Moortele, *The Romantic Overture and Musical Form from Rossini to Wagner* (Cambridge: Cambridge University Press, 2017), 191–221.

36. 'Das Clavier-Concert', 6, col. 2: 'Sebastian Bach sieht an der Harmonieführung hier und da heraus'. These issues are addressed in Macdonald, *Robert Schumann and the Piano Concerto*, 197–212.

37. On the position of the cadenza in post-classical piano concerti, see Robert Gauldin, 'New Twists for Old Endings: Cadenza and Apotheosis in the Romantic Piano Concerto', *Intégral* 18/19 (2004–5): 1–23. Gauldin examines Schuman's cadenza in ibid., 7–8.

38. Robert Schumann, *Tagebüche*, vol. 2: 1836–1854, edited by Gerd Nauhaus (Leipzig: VEB Deutscher Verlag für Musik, 1987), 164, and see also Daverio, *Robert Schumann*, 235.

39. Robert Schumann, *Tagebüche*, vol. 3: 1837–1847, edited by Gerd Nauhaus (Leipzig: VEB Deutscher Verlag für Musik, 1982), 181.

40. Schumann, *Tagebüche*, vol. 2, 164.

41. Schumann, *Tagebüche*, vol. 3, 182–3.

42. Kang, 'Robert Schumann's Piano Concerto in A minor, Op. 54', 13–16 and Wolfgang Boetticher, 'Preface', in Robert Schumann, *Phantasie for Piano and Orchestra in A Minor, WoO*, edited by Wolfgang Boetticher (London: Ernst Eulenburg, 1994), iii–xix, at vi.

43. *Robert Schumanns Briefe: Neue Folge*, edited by Gustav Jensen (Leipzig: Breitkopf und Härtel, 1886), 438 and 444–5, cited in Kang, 'Robert Schumann's Piano Concerto in A Minor, Op. 54', 15 and Daverio, *Robert Schumann*, 312–13.

44. Wolfgang Boetticher, 'Preface', ix–x.

45. Bernhard Appel, 'Kulturgut oder Kapitalanlage? Zum Ankauf des Autographs von Robert Schumanns Klavierkonzert Op. 54', *Neue Zeitschrift für Musik* 151 (1990): 11–12.

46. Ibid.

47. Kang argues that this passage was conceived as a solo transition; see 'Robert Schumann's Piano Concerto in A Minor, Op. 54', 26–8.

48. Boetticher, 'Preface', x. This revision is also considered in Kang, 'Robert Schumann's Piano Concerto in A Minor, Op. 54', 28–9.
49. Boetticher, 'Preface', xiii–xiv.
50. Stephen Roe, 'The Autograph Manuscript of Schumann's Piano Concerto', *Musical Times* 131/1764 (1990): 77–9, at 79. Roe consequently speculates about the extent of Clara's involvement in the composition of the solo part; it seems likely that Robert worked closely with her in its preparation.
51. Bernhard Appel, 'Die Überleitung vom 2. zum 3. Satz in Robert Schumanns Klavierkonzert Opus 54', *Die Musikforschung* 44 (July–September 1991): 255–61, at 257–9.
52. Cited in Joan Chissell, *Clara Schumann: A Dedicated Spirit* (London: Hamish Hamilton, 1983), 95.

3

ANALYSIS (1): THE FIRST MOVEMENT

Sonata Function, Sonata Form and Sonata Cycle

Analysis of the first movement's form is complicated by its dual identity as a stand-alone *Phantasie* and a movement within a concerto cycle. The first movement's conflation of form and cycle noted by Claudia Macdonald and August Gerstmeier is explained in Table 3.1.[1] This is an early, fledgling example of the 'two-dimensional' sonata form that Vande Moortele detects in works by Liszt, Strauss, Schoenberg and Zemlinsky: Schumann composes a sonata, which also houses a first movement, slow movement and finale. To adopt Vande Moortele's terminology, the *andante espressivo* at the start of the development 'identifies' with the slow movement and the coda identifies with the finale, which means that, as movements, these passages paradoxically exist at a lower level of formal hierarchy than the sonata form that contains them. With the advent of Op. 54's second movement, however, this perception is reversed: the cycle of movements now stands *above* the first movement's sonata form, which is no longer the highest level of the formal hierarchy. The movements of the cycle initially function as subdivisions of a sonata form; but after the first movement, sonata form functions as a subdivision of the movement cycle. The *Phantasie*'s design, in short, aspires to a formal condition, which is compromised by Schumann's decision to compose the Intermezzo and rondo. This generates an analytical conundrum which is central to any rich understanding of the work: the first movement is already a cycle of movements in miniature, but once the slow movement is underway, the first movement's cyclic features are, so to speak, demoted, and we have to reappraise its formal contribution as part of a larger movement cycle.

Table 3.1 *Schumann, Op. 54/i, form and cycle*

Bars:	1	4	19⁴	36	67	134	156	185	205	251	259	274⁴	291	320	385	402	458
Cycle:	first movement						slow movement										finale
Form:	exposition						development				recapitulation					cadenza	coda
	intro.	A	TR	B⇔TR	tutti		pre-core 1	pre-core 2	core	RT	A	TR	B⇔TR	tutti			
Key:	V/i	i	→	(III)→	III		♭I	♭I →	VII→	V/i	i	→	(III) →	I		i	

Sonata Function, Sonata Form and Sonata Cycle

Example 3.1 Schumann, Op. 54/i, derivation of *andante espressivo* and *allegro molto* from first theme.

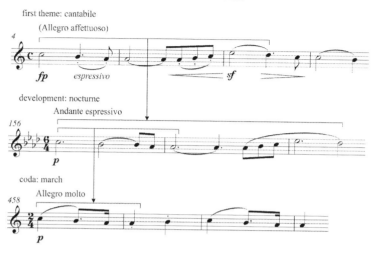

The first movement's two-dimensionality is achieved through a further adjustment of generic expectation, which is implicit in the *Phantasie* but explicit in Op. 54: Schumann rejects the traditional type 5 form bequeathed by the late eighteenth-century concerto in favour of a modified variant of a standard, type 3 sonata. In order to achieve the impression of two-dimensionality, Schumann does not compose new material but presents old music in new expressive guises. More specifically, and as Example 3.1 reveals, both the 'slow movement' and 'finale' derive from the first theme, which they vary not only by modifying some of its melodic properties but more importantly by also changing its *topic*. The *andante espressivo* transforms the *allegro* theme into a nocturne, complete with the style's characteristic flowing left-hand accompaniment; the *allegro molto* contrastingly converts the same theme into a brisk 2/4 march. Schumann, in other words, employs a method of 'cyclical transformation' which anticipates Liszt's symphonic poems of the 1850s: contrasting movements emerge within a single form because variations that change a theme's topical character also change the implied movement type. These 'movements' are not simply interpolations but also have a role in the overarching sonata form, precisely because they are derived from the first theme. The *andante* varies the first theme as part of the development section's thematic action, a process the *allegro molto* carries into the coda.[2]

If Table 3.1 suggests a reasonably clear sonata form for the first movement, detailed examination of the exposition reveals a more complex picture. The movement begins efficiently and unproblematically with a periodic first theme, unambiguously prolonging the tonic A minor shared between an orchestral antecedent (bars 4–11) and a solo consequent (bars 12–19), prefaced by a three-bar introductory flourish; a transition is then clearly signalled on the last beat of bar 19. From this point, however, the exposition's design becomes much harder to interpret; as Stephan Lindeman perceptively observes: 'This piece is one of those few works of art in which the perception of its structural features ... somehow dissolves into the flow of the music.'[3] A modulation to G is accomplished by bar 35, articulated by a recession of texture of the sort normally associated with a medial caesura (MC); that is, the cadential or half-cadential pause, which flags the arrival of a second theme. This impression is reinforced by the music of bars 36–9, which reveals the preceding G major harmony as a dominant and seemingly articulates the start of a theme in C, which, as the relative major, is the second theme's expected tonality (see Example 3.2). Location of the second theme at bar 36 is, however, problematic, for several reasons. First, the music at bar 36 is not new but is an outgrowth of the motive initially established, in the tonic, at bar 26, anacrusis 25. Second, and more seriously, the music from bar 40 does not consolidate this theme or its key, but veers off towards F, initiating a passage that reverts to the textural energy and harmonic mobility of a transition. The impression given is that Schumann has proposed and then rejected a second theme; in effect, the form regresses into a transition from bar 40.

This new transitional action persists until bar 58, where a sequential process of modulation dissipates over vii$^{\mathrm{dim.7}}$/V in C. Having rejected one candidate for an MC, we now seem to be approaching another; or, at least, the arrival on a $^6_4$ chord in bar 59 suggests a new attempt to secure C major and an associated second

Sonata Function, Sonata Form and Sonata Cycle

Example 3.2 Schumann, Op. 54/i, bars 34–41.

theme. As Example 3.3 reveals, Schumann now reinstates the first theme, temporarily indicating that the exposition is really monothematic and the second theme has arrived as a variant of the first, poised over the relative major's dominant. Yet this music is also in transit: properly speaking, the $^6_4$ chord at bar 59 moves to V in bar 66, which in turn resolves to the root-position chord of C at bar 67, which is the progression's true goal. We now perceive that the statement of the first theme initiated at bar 59 functions as an elaboration of V/III, and consequently as preparation for a thematic presentation, not as a presentation as such.

Schumann, in sum, has twice attempted and twice retracted a second theme; and in each case, the sense of thematic presentation is subsumed into transitional processes. Schumann here applies a distinctively Romantic technique, which Janet Schmalfeldt has

Analysis (1)

Example 3.3 Schumann, Op. 54/i, bars 59–69.

termed 'becoming': that is, *'the special case whereby the formal function initially suggested by a musical idea, phrase, or section invites retrospective reinterpretation within the larger formal context'*.[4] I have elsewhere called this practice *functional transformation*, a term that explains situations in which music initially heard to convey one formal function retrospectively takes on another one. Following Vande Moortele and Nathan Martin, I identify three distinctive kinds of functional transformation, which differ depending on the expected order in which functions occur.[5] 'Progressive' transformation concerns situations in which a formal function has to be reinterpreted as its successor, for example when an introduction retrospectively becomes a first theme; Schmalfeldt signifies this with the symbol '⇒'. 'Regressive' transformation describes the opposite: a function is subsequently reinterpreted as its predecessor, signified with the symbol '⇐': for example, second theme ⇐ transition. Finally, 'circular' transformation occurs when music oscillates repeatedly between two functions, described using the symbol '⇔'. This is what happens in bars 19–66: second theme ⇔ transition.

This oscillation comes to an end at bar 67, thanks to the clear structural downbeat and categorical arrival in C major. Yet this stabilisation does not dispel formal ambiguity for very long. On the one hand, the tonal consolidation at bar 67 supports the return of the first theme, presented as if it were a stable second theme in C in the manner of a monothematic exposition, which discloses two phrase-structural units. The first is a large sentence, consisting of a statement (bars 67–70), response (bars 71–6), continuation (bars 77–84) and perfect authentic cadence in G (bars 85–7), which the standing on V in bars 87–94 immediately reinterprets as a half-cadence in C. The second unit begins in bar 95 by returning to the statement and response introduced in bars 67–76, but in bar 102 Schumann supplies a new continuation, constructed from the discarded second theme first adumbrated in bars 25–7, which dissolves over a half-cadence in bar 111. A graduated intensification process begins tentatively in bar 112, leading to a half-cadence in bar 131 and the triumphal consolidation of C established with the tutti entry in bar 134.

On the other hand, the soloist's flowing quaver triplets, which pervade the texture from bar 67 until the exposition's end, lend all of this music the character of a display episode, and thereby give the impression that bar 67 initiates a closing section, not a second theme. Rhetorically, both of these functions are implied throughout this passage; yet we only realise that it must be the closing section as well as the second theme once the tutti has commenced and no separate closing section is forthcoming. Consequently, whereas in bars 19–66 potential second themes are continually folded back into transitional action, after bar 67 the delayed second theme coexists with the closing function that it ordinarily precedes. To put this another way, from the perspective of the exposition's end, the second theme 'becomes', which is to say retrospectively transforms into, the closing section. Expressed symbolically: in bars 19–66, second theme ⇔ transition; in bars 67–134, second theme ⇒ closing section.

In form-functional terms, the development and recapitulation are to varying degrees less problematic. The recapitulation brings back the exposition in full but modifies its tonal scheme in the transition, between bars 296 and 302, so that the music ultimately returns to the tonic major, an event that Hepokoski and Darcy call the 'crux'.[6] Example 3.4 compares this passage with the corresponding music in the exposition. Schumann's first attempt at a second theme recurs from bar 291, and initially in the same

Example 3.4 Schumann, Op. 54/i, comparison of bars 41–67 and 296–312.

key, but the tonal parallelism goes awry in bar 296 because the pianist's scalar descent, which in the exposition resolves as a dominant seventh of F, is diverted at the last minute onto an F sharp, which is then interpreted as V of B minor, in which key the

Example 3.4 (cont.)

orchestra's tempestuous interjection is now reprised, and a series of distortions of the expositional model ensue. The sequential passage in bars 48–56 is then replicated, but truncated through the omission of two bars, which means that it now starts and ends in the same place (A minor in bar 302 leads to A major in bar 312). From here to the tutti at the recapitulation's end, there is complete correspondence with the exposition, but now transposed into A major. The recapitulation recalls all of the formal ambiguities and manifold processes of becoming that characterise the exposition; and yet it is qualitatively and experientially different, precisely because it revisits and glosses the exposition. The circular and progressive transformations are still perceived, but now as variants of a process we have experienced and can anticipate.

The development conveys none of the ambiguity that besets the exposition. The *andante espressivo* is, to be sure, a major factor in promoting the impression of two-dimensionality. Form-functionally, its claim to be a slow movement rests not only on its expressive character but also on its thematic and tonal self-containment, as an expanded sentential design that opens and closes in the same key: statement in bars 156–9; response in bars 160–3; two stages of continuation in bars 164–70 and 171–8; and a cadential phrase, closing with a perfect authentic cadence (PAC), in bars 179–84, elided with the start of the next section in 185. As part of the form rather than the cycle, it is the first of two 'pre-core' sections; the second follows in bar 185 and restores the material of the introduction, employing it sequentially to modulate towards G major, in which key the core begins in bar 205. From this point, Schumann employs a developmental technique, which he also deploys in the symphonies and chamber music: a large model-sequence-fragmentation scheme is established (in bars 205–28) and then repeated and varied (in bars 229–50) before the music finds the dominant in preparation for the recapitulation (in bar 251).

Despite its distinct topical character, the coda differs from the *andante* in that its harmonic and phrase-structural conventions are wholly cadential or post-cadential and therefore more consistent with a codetta or closing section than a self-contained movement. It comprises three large phrase units, bars 458–89, 490–516[1] and 516–44. Bars 458–89 and 490–516[1] are based on expanded cadential progressions, which are first evaded and then closed as PACs and supplied with their own post-cadential phrase extensions; bars 516–44 are entirely post-cadential and function as the movement's final tonic prolongation. In consequence, the coda's claim to be a movement as well as a formal function is less secure than that of the *andante espressivo* because it lacks presentational integrity. As William Caplin might say, its music projects an 'after-the-end' function, which means that its status as a distinct movement rests more heavily on the new topical features it introduces.[7]

At the same time, the coda is implicated in a structural process that stretches back into the exposition, which gives its cadential progressions additional formal significance. The modal trajectory of the recapitulation and coda plays out a variant of what Hepokoski and Darcy call 'sonata failure' because the return of the second group in the tonic major, which signals a positive expressive transformation of the movement's minor mode, is undone by the cadenza, which depresses the modality back to A minor, a negative outcome, which the coda confirms. Moreover, the recapitulation's A major music has an underlying structural weakness, which is that it never really achieves a secure PAC that clinches A major. The closest we get to this is the cadential progression leading into the tutti's return in bars 381–5, which is an imperfect rather than a perfect authentic cadence, or IAC (its soprano line

Example 3.5 Schumann, Op. 54/i, bass diagram.

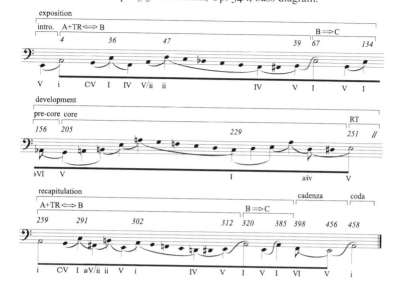

reaches $\hat{3}$ rather than $\hat{1}$ when the tonic arrives in bar 385). This insecurity is seeded in the exposition: the corresponding progression in bars 128–34 leads initially to a half-cadence, the dominant of which is separated from the tutti's tonic by the pianist's two-bar expansion of V/III before the orchestra enters. Transposition of the exposition's second group and tutti into the tonic major produces a comparable structural issue. In the language of sonata theory, the key cadences in the exposition and recapitulation, which Hepokoski and Darcy call the essential expositional closure (EEC) and the essential structural closure (ESC)., are structurally insufficient. The coda's cadences secure what the recapitulation lacks – a PAC in the tonic – but this closure comes at a cost because Schumann abandons the tonic major in order to achieve it.

Example 3.5 overlays all this formal information onto a reduction of the movement's underlying bass progression, which reveals key aspects of the movement's tonal design. The apparent extremism of Schumann's sudden turn from C major to

B minor at the recapitulatory 'crux' in bars 295–302, for instance, becomes explicable as one element of a conjunct bass descent C–B–A, each stage of which is supplied with its own preparatory dominant. Example 3.5 also exposes the structural role of bass neighbour notes at two critical formal junctures. First, although the *andante espressivo*'s A flat tonality has no function in the context of A minor, Example 3.5 shows that it is really an elaboration of a chromatic neighbour note to G: the exposition concludes in C; the *andante* begins in A flat; and the development core starts in G. The structural progression here is the move from C to its dominant, to which the A flat is appended as a chromatic prefix. The development core then works its way back towards the home dominant in preparation for the recapitulation, via alternating stepwise and fourth-based progressions: bars 205–17 ascend by step from G to B; bars 217–21 are built around the fourth progression B–E–A; transposition of this whole process beginning on C at bar 229 brings the music to D by bar 245, which in turn slips by chromatic step up to E at bar 251, where the retransition takes hold.

The second crucial use of a bass upper-neighbour note comes in the cadenza, which engineers a huge expansion of VI as a neighbour to the dominant of A minor. As Example 3.6 explains, this happens at several structural levels. On the largest scale, the cadenza is framed by a bass F, beginning with the German augmented sixth in bars 398–402, which releases the soloist from their accompanimental role in the A major tutti, and ending with the prolongation of F major in bars 452–5, spanning a four-octave bass descent, which precedes the arrival of V at the cadenza's end. Internally, the cadenza plays out a conflict between F as neighbour to V and F as temporary tonic. The bass F of bars 398–402 moves to E in bar 403, coordinated with the decay of A major to A minor, and bars 403–17 work to secure A minor, culminating in the approach to a tonic PAC in 417. This cadence is, however, interrupted by VI in the next bar, and by bar 420 F major has been categorically reasserted. F again becomes the root of a German augmented sixth in bar 433, resolving in an orthodox manner to a V^6_4 in the following bar, above which the first theme returns in A minor. Again, however, there is a sustained drift towards F,

Example 3.6 Schumann, Op. 54/i, cadenza, VI–V relations.

which is fulfilled once V^6_5/F is reached in bar 451. This tendency is decisively quashed in bars 454–6, where F is reinterpreted as the root of an augmented sixth for the final time and resolved onto V in preparation for the coda. Altogether, the cadenza nests VI–V relations such that attempts to make F function as a neighbour to the dominant rather than vice versa are repeatedly undermined. The coda's A minor PACs also respond to this local drama by stabilising the tonic in the aftermath of F's repeated intrusions.

Thematic Process and the 'Symphonic' Concerto

As we have seen, one claim made frequently on Op. 54's behalf is that all this formal innovation nominates the work as a seminal example of the symphonic concerto. In addition to the decision to employ a type 3 sonata, the first movement's symphonism is located most tangibly in its thematic and motivic construction: by eschewing the marked formal and topical separation of the virtuoso concerto in favour of a more fluid, economical and formally evasive rotation through a limited pool of motives, Schumann achieves a kind of coherence more commonly associated with symphonies than with concerti.

Several attempts have been made to map and classify the first movement's thematic relationships. Macdonald reduces its diversity to three themes and their variations, appraised in Example 3.7.[8] The first theme yields a in Macdonald's terminology; the transition introduces b; and the introduction contributes x. Transformations of a and b account for the vast bulk of the movement's material. Crucially, these transformations supervene the schematic aspects of the sonata form because there is no distinct association of motive and sonata function: a serves as both first and second themes; b is deployed as a counterpart to a in the transition, as a contrasting idea in the second group, and as the material of the exposition's closing tutti.

As Macdonald illustrates, the development and coda subject a to both variation and topical transformation by changing the motive's expressive character and supplying it with new continuations. The treatment of a across the movement reveals a discernible strategy, based on the idea that association with the first theme should be reduced increasingly to a alone. As Example 3.5 explains, the *andante espressivo*'s transformation of the first theme into a $\frac{6}{4}$ nocturne discontinues the theme's original form midway through its contrasting idea. The core of the development, commencing at bar 205, further reduces the correspondence: a is present, but the material deviates thereafter. Finally, the martial variant of the first theme that underpins the coda consists solely of a; all other first-theme correspondences are discarded.

The treatment of b initially travels in the opposite direction: starting off life as a kind of motivic 'stem' in the exposition's transition, it gradually accrues new continuations, summarised in Example 3.7. It is first extended by means of melodic sequencing, producing the variant heard from bar 32, which then supplies the material of bars 32–47. A further melodic extension of the motive generates the *espressivo* form arising at bar 102, which is then

Example 3.7 Schumann, Op. 54/i, motives in Macdonald's analysis.

motive *a* and its variants (Macdonald 2005)

transformed into a heroic, major-mode counterpart in the tutti that intervenes at bar 133.

The fates of *a* and *b* entwine in the cadenza, which serves motivically as a kind of second development. It begins with an idea Macdonald describes as a 'retrograde' of *b* (*b1*), although this connection is loose at best; perhaps the only verifiable relationship

Example 3.7 (cont.)

with *b* is a commonality of rhythm, for which reason I have labelled it *y* in Example 3.7. After this, the development of *y* proceeds in three stages, each of which concludes with a process of liquidation: that is, its reduction to a remaining melodic 'residue', as Schoenberg described it.[9] Bars 402–18 spin out *y* towards the deceptive cadence in bars 417–18, which retains its second half and discards the first. A second stage begins in bar 419 with a new variant of *y*, labelled *y1* in Example 3.7, which is subject to sequential treatment in bars 419–25 and fragments as the $^6_4$ chord in bar 434 approaches. The dominant attained at this point heralds a third stage based initially on *a*, which is also subject to sequential treatment and is liquidated towards the cadenza's concluding trill in bars 456–7, where *y* makes its final appearance.

Motive *x* is the movement's most sparsely employed idea, providing the substance of the introduction and the linking material between the end of the *andante espressivo* and the development's core. Again, the process acting on *x* has a discernible logic: it is first of all installed as the model of a sequential progression in bars 185–6, which is duly sequenced in 187–92 and then fragmented in bars 193–6. Ingeniously, the eight bars leading into the return of first-theme material from bar 197 then transform *x* into an adumbration of *y*.

A second sense in which Op. 54's thematic procedure appears as 'symphonic' is in its use of cyclical techniques. This is most obvious in *a*'s intervention in the transition from the Intermezzo to the Finale, which we will consider in more detail in Chapter 4. Juan Martin Koch has also called attention to *y*'s reappearance at the end of the Intermezzo, quoted in Example 3.7, as the movement's A reprise dissolves towards the transition into the Finale.[10] Other inter-movement connections are at best subcutaneous, at worst fortuitous or accidental. Koch, for example, suggests that the theme with which the first-movement transition begins, which I call *z* in Example 3.7, supplies the framework for the Finale's second theme. More tenuously, Gerstmeier posits that the first themes of all three movements are related by a shared stepwise melodic ascent, and moreover that the melodic contour of the Finale's first theme is arrived at by retrograding *a*.[11] These connections range from the plausible to the speculative; at the very least, they indicate a desire to associate movements by allusion, and to suggest inter-movement connections through the strategic use of melodic similarity.

Yet the first movement is also qualitatively different from the Intermezzo and rondo, in neither of which do we find the same degree of misalignment between theme, function and form. In this respect, the most remarkable aspect of the first movement is not its motivic economy but the fact that there is no strict alignment of motivic material and the progress of the sonata form's contrasted thematic functions. Both first and second themes are variants built from *a*; and *b*, as the primary agent of material contrast, only affiliates with second-theme function fleetingly via its putative second-theme status in bar 36, which is immediately undone as the music regresses into a transition. Appropriating Hepokoski and Darcy's term, the motivic design of the exposition, and by extension of the recapitulation, is better understood as comprising two 'rotations' – that is, cycles through the ordering of the material – the second of which begins once C major is secured as the exposition's closing key. Altogether, we can under-stand the exposition as projecting a counterpoint between two parameters – the motivic-thematic material and the progression of formal functions – which align at the exposition's midpoint to articulate the arrival of C major, but which are otherwise in conflict. The multiple instances of 'becoming' described here and the sense of a dissolution of form 'into the flow of the music' noted by Lindeman are the formal effects of this parametric duality.

Virtuosity and Lyricism

Although all of this departs ostensibly from the conventions of the virtuoso concerto, closer inspection reveals that Schumann retains many of the virtuoso style's hallmarks but subtly integrates them into his type 3 design. This is readily apparent at the Concerto's opening, quoted up to bar 21 in Example 3.8; comparison with the solo entries shown in Examples 1.1, 1.2 and 1.3 in Chapter 1 clarifies Schumann's debt. His introduction, first theme and tran-sition project exactly the bravura–nocturne–*brillante* solo-entry topical succession, which Chapter 1 identified as fundamental to

Example 3.8 Schumann, Op. 54, bravura–cantabile episode display scheme mapped onto introduction, first theme and transition.

the virtuoso style: the introduction's chordal flourish references a bravura preface; the theme itself suggests a cantabile style; and the continuous semiquavers of the transition beginning in bar 19 imply *brillante* or display. Comparing this sequence with the way Herz introduces his soloist in his Op. 34, the work on which Schumann modelled his unfinished concerto of 1830–1, shows that Herz deploys the same topical division of labour. Following an eight-bar bravura flourish, Herz's pianist also turns to a keyboard nocturne. With the tonic PAC articulating the transition's start, Herz then shifts to the running semiquavers indicative of a display episode. Schumann's topical succession – two modes of virtuosity framing a vocal episode – is also Herz's, even though Herz composes a type 5 sonata and Schumann does not.

Schumann also preserves the bravura–nocturne–*brillante* succession's projection across the form as a whole: the first movement is distinctive not because it rejects these stylistic attributes but because it repurposes them for the type 3 sonata. Table 3.2 traces their distribution across the first movement. It is immediately clear that the threefold topical discourse present in the introduction, first theme and transition also spans the exposition. The display material introduced from bar 19 dissipates from bar 31, but the reduced piano texture is short-lived and yields to bravura octaves from bar 39. The first theme's return at bar 59 recovers its cantabile idiom, and display is decisively reinstalled from bar 67. The development covers the same topical ground: the pre-core begins with a nocturne, thereby referencing the habit of including a cantabile pre-core common to dozens of virtuoso concerti; the return of the introduction material from bar 185 is also the return of its bravura topic; and the development core and retransition occupying bars 205–58 revert to the modes of display apparent in bars 67–133, enclosing rapid triplet figuration in material developed out of the first theme. The recapitulation is a full reprise of the exposition, and as such reproduces its succession of topics; and the coda maintains display as the interior of the first theme's martial transformation. The cadenza traverses similar topical terrain. It begins with an imitative texture loosely redolent of the learned style, but by bar 420 this has decisively ceded to bravura; and from bar 434, the first theme's singing style is brought into conversation with *brillante* figuration.

In addition to their redistribution across a type 3 sonata, Schumann's application of virtuoso topics is additionally innovative in that it supports rather than determines the thematic material. More specifically, Schumann often treats virtuosity as the textural interior of a thematic event or process. In this respect, comparison with Kalkbrenner's Concerto No. 4 is instructive. Example 3.9 compares bars 67–70 in Op. 54's first movement with the start of Kalkbrenner's expositional closing section.[12] Both Schumann and Kalkbrenner mobilise continuous piano figuration: semiquavers for Kalkbrenner; quaver triplets for Schumann. But whereas

Table 3.2 Schumann, Op. 54/i, form and topical discourse

Bars:	1	4	19⁴	36	67	156	185	205
Form:	exposition					development		
	intro.	A	TR	B⇔TR	B⇒C	pre-core		core+RT
Topic:	bravura	cantabile	*brillante*	cantabile/bravura	*brillante*	cantabile (nocturne)	bravura	*brillante*

Bars:	259	274⁴	291	320	402	485
Form:	recapitulation				cadenza	coda
	A	TR	B⇔TR	B⇒C		
Topic:	cantabile	*brillante*	cantabile/bravura	*brillante*	learned style→bravura→cantabile	*brillante* (march)

Example 3.9 Schumann, Op. 54/i and Kalkbrenner, Op. 127/i, comparison of closing sections.

Kalkbrenner treats the figuration as form-defining – it *is* the closing section's characteristic material – Schumann's *brillante* topic is entirely accompanimental, supplying the interior of a texture, the exterior of which is the clarinet's recovery of motive *a*. In fact, this is Schumann's strategy throughout the movement, occurring wherever virtuoso concerti would typically locate *brillante* figuration: the transition and closing section in the exposition and recapitulation; the core of the development; and the coda.

The idea that Schumann's objective is to repurpose and integrate inherited stylistic features, rather than to replace them or favour some over others, also helps us to reconcile Macdonald's, Juan Martin Koch's and Gerstmeier's perspectives on motivic coherence with Dahlhaus' views that the source of Op. 54's novelty is the lyric piano piece, and that the music's coherence is consequently a product of its textural rather than its motivic integrity, reflecting an origin in Schumann's lyric piano style of the 1830s. Viewed from Dahlhaus' perspective, it is clear that the piano writing in bars 67–134 owes a debt to the lyric character piece's tendency towards textural uniformity. The whole of the closing section could reasonably audition as an expanded song without words, in which the melody shifts between the winds and the piano's right hand, beneath which the pianist maintains a stylistically characteristic arpeggiated accompaniment. The result, however, is an amalgamation of styles rather than a privileging of the lyric style. Because the soloist is free to expand the texture while the winds convey the principal material, they can also develop the lyric figuration to the point where it intersects with virtuoso display. This is exactly what happens: Schumann makes the closing section's textural interior do the job of a display episode and a lyric piano texture *at the same time*. And since they support a transformation of the first theme, they also facilitate a motivic process, which lends the music a symphonic as well as a concerted dimension.

Schumann's most overt nod to the character piece, however, comes with the *andante espressivo*, which resembles the corresponding passage in Field's Concerto No. 7 to an extent that surely transcends coincidence.[13] Example 3.10 compares the two passages. As we saw in Chapter 1, both passages are nocturnes appearing, in a slower tempo, at the same formal juncture. Both arrive via a modulation away from the exposition's tonal terminus, albeit more radically in Schumann's case (Field simply progresses from III to V via v). More remarkably, both facilitate a developmental treatment of the move-ment's first theme by transforming its topic; and both themes grow from the same melodic figure, which is a $\hat{3}$–$\hat{2}$–$\hat{1}$ descent. As Example 3.10 explains, the relationship is a little more obscure in Field's case, thanks to the dotted, siciliana-like figure with which he embellishes $\hat{2}$. The point here is not simply that Field and Schumann have imported a lyric miniature into a concerto but that they have

Example 3.10 Schumann, Op. 54 and Field, Concerto No. 7, comparison of nocturne episodes.

exploited an existing feature of the virtuoso concerto – the tendency to start the development with a 'cantabile section', as Schumann himself described it – in order to engineer a kind of synthesis of the concerto and the character piece. Here also there is no inconsistency with Op. 54's symphonic tendencies because the confluence of concerto and character piece contributes to the movement's motivic economy: a topical transformation of the first theme permits the integration of generic precursors.

Dialogue, Texture and Cultural Politics

Perhaps the most obvious difference between Schumann's first movement and its forebears is its radical rethinking of the dialogue between soloist and orchestra, which for much of the movement resembles neither the virtuoso concerto nor its Mozartian antecedents. Superficially, this is attributable to the presence of a type 3 rather than a type 5 sonata, in which respect Schumann's debt to

Mendelssohn's Opp. 25 and 40 is readily apparent. But the inter-action of form, topic and thematic process mapped earlier adds layers of complexity to the solo–orchestral interactions, which Mendelssohn's first movements lack, the key to which is the way the thematic material is distributed between pianist and orchestra.

In one sense, Schumann's approach is closer to Mozart than it is to Herz in that it overtly rekindles the Mozartian ideals of collaboration and dialogue stressed by Keefe, moving con-sciously away from the textural dualities of the virtuoso con-certo. At the same time, Schumann also differs essentially from Mozart because the dramatic dialogue at which Mozart aims is nevertheless defined by the overarching distinction between ritornelli and solo episodes, which no amount of dialogic inter-action ever displaces. In the first movement of Op. 54, however, this distinction is almost entirely absent, not only thanks to the lack of a type 5 sonata but also because the orchestra almost never acts independently. There is only one fully fledged tutti, at the exposition's end; and as we saw in Chapter 2, the removal of the piano at this point was a later decision, meaning that in the *Phantasie*'s original conception the orchestra did not substan-tially punctuate the form at any juncture.

Table 3.3 clarifies Schumann's approach to solo–orchestral interaction by tracking the instrumental ownership of a and b across the first movement's form. Crucially, neither the soloist nor the orchestra ever has total possession of the material, and the ways in which it is disposed are in constant transformation. Specifically, the instrumental disposition of the two ideas is stra-tegically distinct to the point where we can reasonably argue that the form is underpinned by a textural duality. The narrative of motive a is entirely a matter of how piano and winds interact, with the rest of the orchestra playing a supporting role. Motive a is initially articulated by textural opposition, since the first-theme antecedent is given to the wind group and the consequent to the piano. The remaining treatment of a subtly balances or diffuses the first group's division of labour. In bar 59, the pianist alone picks up a, while in the second group, a returns to the winds, which the piano now accompanies. The development then explores two modes of textural interaction that do not occur in the exposition.

Table 3.3 Schumann, Op. 54/i, instrumental distribution of 'a' and 'b'

Bars:	4	12	25⁴	32	36	42	59	67	102⁴
Form:	exposition								
	first group		TR				second group/closing section		
'a'	winds alone	piano alone	-	piano	strings	tutti alone	piano alone	solo winds	-
'b'	-	-	strings/winds	-	-	-	-	-	wind/piano alternation

Bars:	134	156	205	259	267	280⁴	287	290	297
Form:	development			recapitulation					
		pre-core (andante)	core	first group		TR			
'a'	piano/solo wind alternation		piano doubling solo winds	winds alone	piano alone	strings/winds	piano	strings	tutti alone
'b'	tutti alone	-	-	-	-	-	-	-	-

Bars:	312	320	355⁴	385	402	434	458
Form:	second group/closing section				cadenza		coda
'a'	piano alone	solo winds	-	tutti with solo accompaniment	-	piano alone	winds with solo accompaniment
'b'	-	-	wind/piano alternation	tutti with solo accompaniment	piano alone ('b' variant 'y')	-	-

Initially, the *andante espressivo* alternates iterations of *a* between piano and winds above a consistent nocturne accompaniment; and the development core from bar 205 allows soloist and winds, for the first and only time, to convey *a* by doubling. With the arrival of the recapitulation, these two instrumental groups are separated out again. Finally, the cadenza and coda articulate two polarised approaches to piano–wind interaction because the soloist alone conveys *a* in the cadenza, whereas in the coda the entire wind group homophonically shares *a* while the pianist accompanies.

Piano–wind alternation is also one feature of *b*'s treatment; but a much more prominent strategy in *b*'s case is to involve the strings while the soloist accompanies or drops out, or else to displace or subsume the soloist with the tutti, neither of which choices of instrumentation are ever applied to *a*. The exceptions are the interjection of *b* at bar 102 in the second group/closing section and the corresponding point in the recapitulation from bar 355, which are the only formal locations in which winds and piano collaborate to present *b*, a decision that establishes a marked contrast with *b*'s treatment in the transition and closing tutti. The cadenza in effect functions as a kind of textural portal between the worlds of *a* and *b*, as well as a locus of development, because it begins by following up the tutti assertion of *b* with its related variant *y*, which is then liquidated and replaced by *a* in bars 431–4, after which *b* plays no further formal role.

These strategies suggest socio-political resonances for Op. 54 which have no obvious precedent in classical or virtuoso models. The Enlightenment ideal of rational dialogue between individual and collective that Keefe observes in Mozart operates within a formal framework that ultimately preserves the solo–orchestral dichotomy: however the piano and orchestra converse in the solo episodes, the orchestra almost always has the first and last word. Virtuoso concerti retain this framing, but their internal elevation of the pianist produces a form in which the orchestral collective is otherwise mostly reduced to a condition of subservience. Schumann rejects both social orders: the pianist is neither a rational voice to which the collective pays benevolent attention nor a heroic figure to whom the collective submits. Rather, the soloist is sometimes deployed as an orchestral instrument, sometimes the orchestra is used to augment the piano's texture and at other times Schumann establishes a kind of chamber-musical core, primarily involving the piano and winds, which the strings support, but the net effect is that no participant gains any ultimate advantage. Moreover, because the texture is distributed in service of the thematic material's progress, and above all the dual narratives unfolding around *a* and *b*, all participants refer to a higher, abstract musical entity, which as we have seen is not congruent with the articulation of sonata-form functions.

The result is a kind of aesthetic community, akin to the 'pedagogical province' imagined by Goethe in Book II of *Wilhelm Meisters Wanderjahre*, which envisions a state in which musical tuition underpins the formation of society. For Goethe, the pedagogical province's highest ideals are embodied in the symphony, in which, as Mark Evan Bonds explains, 'No soloist dominates, and every instrument contributes its own distinctive and indispensable sound to the larger whole.'[14] Musical instruction, in this context, facilitates *Bildung*: it is simultaneously a vehicle for personal, social and political formation, the goal of which is the ability to partake of symphonic performance as the highest form of socio-musical participation. Opus 54 is, of course, a concerto, not a symphony; but the notion of collaboration that underpins the first movement is patently redolent of Goethe's socio-symphonic ideal.

Goethe's allegory also chimes readily with Schumann's progressive politics, on which Celia Applegate has discerned two essential influences.[15] The first is a fusion of post-Kantian Enlightenment rationalism, which installs the rationally autonomous individual as the central political agent in society, with a geographically rooted nationalism, in which the exercise of rational freedom helps to bind communities that share a sense of place. The second is a recognition of the public sphere, defined by Jürgen Habermas as a space for rational discourse that is independent of monarchic or clerical influence, as the incubator of cultural progress and national consciousness.[16] Applegate quotes the prospectus Schumann wrote for the *Neue Zeitschrift* in 1834 by way of evidence, in particular its voicing of the need 'to create for the artist an organ which would stimulate him to effectiveness, not only through his direct influence, but also through the printed and spoken word, *a public place*, for him to express what he has seen with his own eyes, and felt with his own spirit'. The journal, for Schumann, carved out a public forum for autonomous artistic discourse, which might nurture a specifically German aesthetic spirit, dedicated to a kind of localised cultural renewal. As Applegate explains: 'The issue was not just people and music ... but people and music in particular places. Musical improvement happened in these places, in cities, which had to be transformed from the places in which aristocrats, philistines and *Salonmenschen* ruled to the sites of musical and cultural renewal.' Schumann was, in other words,

> trying to remake a map of central Europe from an assortment of commercial sites and *Residenzstädte*, dominated by court and purely commercial musical establishments, into a genuinely national network of true *Bürgerstädte*, cities of autonomous, self-governing, self-regulating citizens, in which a new kind of cultural life ... would replace both the old *and* the degraded new or contemporary.[17]

The geographical specificity of Schumann's political-aesthetic vision reflects the political fragmentation of the German lands prior to their unification under Bismarck in 1871. Schumann was a resident of the Kingdom of Saxony from his birth in 1810 until his move to Düsseldorf in 1850. Before 1806, Saxony was an electorate of the Holy Roman Empire, a loose assemblage of petty states and kingdoms under the purview of the Habsburg Emperor in Vienna. After 1806, Saxony was annexed to Napoleon's First French Empire and raised to the status of a kingdom within the patchwork of political entities that collectively formed the Confederation of the Rhine, which included four other kingdoms (Prussia, Bavaria, Westphalia and Württemberg), four grand duchies, thirteen duchies and sixteen principalities. Following Napoleon's defeat at the Battle of Leipzig in 1813, Saxony fell within the German Confederation. Only with Bismarck's victory in the Franco-Prussian War of 1871 was the German Confederation unified into the German Empire under Wilhelm I.[18]

All of this political complexity inflects the cultural circumstances that produced Schumann's Piano Concerto. The forms of German nationalism it sediments echo a geographical consciousness, which, as Applegate describes it, was 'profoundly anticentrist' in that it constructed notions of German identity on a place-specific foundation of cultural growth and advancement.[19] Thus the German liberals of Schumann's time 'were nationalists, not because they paraded around with their German flags, but because they shared belief that the advance of culture meant a transition from communities of people based merely on blood ties and extended kinship to communities of people who were self-consciously connected to places and capable of forming more and more complex participatory states'.[20]

It is not difficult to see how Schumann's aspirations for the piano concerto align with the political mentality Applegate describes; nor is it hard to grasp Op. 54's approach to solo–orchestral interaction as an attempt to give these objectives aesthetic substance. Understood in this light, the first movement of Op. 54 auditions as a political allegory that is aspirational within its time and place. Schumann's pianist is an actor in the public sphere who at once has rational autonomy in that they are at liberty to advance independent assertions about the musical material, and also collective responsibility, since they willingly and routinely collaborate with the orchestra. Unlike the virtuoso type 5 sonata, which locks soloist and orchestra into formally delineated roles, Schumann's flexible type 3 sonata offers no barrier to the interpenetration of individual and collective. In this environment, all instruments pursue the same ideal, which is the generation of form from a shared fund of musical ideas.

Notes

1. Macdonald, 'Mit einer eignen außerordentlichen Composition', 253–5 and Gerstmeier, *Robert Schumann: Klavierkonzert A-moll, Op. 54*, 25.
2. Margaret Fox has interpreted the slow movement and finale as interpolated episodes evidencing the hybridisation of concerto and fantasy; see Fox, 'Deciphering the Arabesque', 163–7.
3. Stephan D. Lindeman, *Structural Novelty and Tradition in the Early Romantic Piano Concerto*, 154.

4. Janet Schmalfeldt, *In the Process of Becoming: Analytic and Philosophical Perspectives on Form in Early Nineteenth-Century Music* (New York: Oxford University Press, 2011), 9.

5. See Julian Horton, 'Rethinking Sonata Failure: Mendelssohn's Overture *Zum Märchen von der schönen Melusine*', *Music Theory Spectrum* 43/2 (2021): 299–319, at 305, and Nathan Martin and Steven Vande Moortele, 'Formal Functions and Retrospective Reinterpretation in the First Movement of Schubert's String Quintet', *Music Analysis* 33/2 (2014): 130–55.

6. Hepokoski and Darcy, *Elements of Sonata Theory*, 239–42.

7. William E. Caplin, 'What Are Formal Functions?', in Pieter Bergé, ed., *Musical Form, Forms and Formenlehre: Three Methodological Reflections* (Leuven: Leuven University Press, 2010), 21–40, at 25–7.

8. Macdonald, *Robert Schumann and the Piano Concerto*, 230–1.

9. Arnold Schoenberg, *Fundamentals of Musical Composition*, edited by Gerald Strang (London: Faber and Faber, 1967), 59–60, where Schoenberg comments that, as a result of the process of motivic liquidation, 'Often only residues remain, which have little in common with the basic motive.'

10. Koch, *Das Klavierkonzert des 19. Jahrhunderts und der Kategorie des Symphonischen*, 215.

11. Gerstmeier, *Robert Schumann: Klavierkonzert A-moll, Op. 54*, 33. A similar analysis is also attempted in Michael Thomas Roeder, *A History of the Concerto* (Portland, OR: Amadeus Press, 1994), 252–4.

12. For a comparison of these two passages, see Julian Horton, *Brahms' Piano Concerto No. 2, Op. 83: Analytical and Contextual Studies* (Leuven: Peeters, 2017), 107–8.

13. On the relationship between Op. 54 and Field's Concerto No. 7 at this point, see Julian Horton, 'John Field and the Alternative History of Concerto First-Movement Form', *Music & Letters* 92/1 (2011): 43–83, at 70–9.

14. Mark Evan Bonds, *Music As Thought: Listening to the Symphony in the Age of Beethoven* (Princeton, NJ: Princeton University Press, 2006), 76; Goethe's pedagogical province is considered in 75–8. As Bonds points out, Goethe's view of the symphony as an allegory of political community was widely shared in post-Enlightenment musical discourse; Bonds, for example, cites Heinrich Christoph Koch and Gottfried Wilhelm Fink.

15. Celia Applegate, 'Robert Schumann and the Culture of German Nationhood', in Roe-Min Kok and Laura Tunbridge, *Rethinking Schumann* (New York: Oxford University Press, 2011), 3–14, at 8–9. Applegate has developed this analysis of Schumann's political

consciousness in *The Necessity of Music: Variations on a German Theme* (Toronto: University of Toronto Press, 2017), 155–66, in the context of a cultural history of music in Germany from the Enlightenment to the later twentieth century. For a review of *Vormärz*-era cultural politics moving beyond Goethe's 'Weimar classicism', see James Garratt, *Music, Culture and Social Reform in the Age of Wagner* (Cambridge: Cambridge University Press, 2010), 44–83.

16. Jürgen Habermas, *The Structural Transformation of the Public Sphere: An Enquiry into a Category of Bourgeois Society* (Cambridge: Polity Press, 1989).

17. Applegate, 'Robert Schumann and the Culture of German Nationhood', 11.

18. Perspectives on regionalism and Saxon history after 1830 are collected in Retallack, ed., *Saxony in German History.*

19. Applegate, 'Robert Schumann and the Culture of German Nationhood', 11.

20. Applegate, *The Necessity of Music*, 161.

4

ANALYSIS (2): THE SLOW MOVEMENT AND RONDO FINALE

The *Phantasie* and the Three-Movement Concerto

The analytical dilemma posed by Schumann's expansion of the *Phantasie* of 1841 into the Concerto of 1845 can be sourced to a contradiction. On the one hand, Schumann conceived the single-movement *Phantasie* as a response to the generic shortcomings of the virtuoso concerto's multi-movement cycle, which the *Phantasie* overcomes by integrating that repertoire's topical hallmarks and movement types into a single-movement that prioritises material development over display or topical discourse. On the other hand, Op. 54 is a three-movement concerto, which means that the first movement's impression of integrative two-dimensionality is qualified as soon as the Intermezzo begins. Consequently, the first movement both is and is not self-contained, and this paradox is intrinsic to Op. 54's compositional genesis. The point is made succinctly by Bernhard Appel, for whom the work engenders 'a kind of formal pleonasm: a concerto within a concerto'.[1]

For both Appel and Daverio, the key to understanding this issue is the transition between the Intermezzo and the Finale. As Chapter 2 explained, the Intermezzo's material fragments without a decisive cadence in the movement's F major tonality and instead drifts towards a half-cadence in A minor by bar 98. Schumann then twice recalls the first movement's motive *a*, in A major and in A minor, in bars 103–6, before major-mode reiterations of this motive propel the music into the Finale. This gesture is bidirectional: looking backwards, the first-movement recall returns us briefly to the world of the *Phantasie*; looking forwards, it facilitates the Finale's inception. The passage's modal indeterminacy underscores the effect, in part by referencing a symphonic rather than a concerted device, which is the minor–major struggle–victory trajectory paradigmatically exemplified by the linkage of Scherzo and Finale in Beethoven's Symphony No. 5. When A major decays to A minor in bars 105–6, the motive's 'positive' major-mode transformation is temporarily undone, suggesting a reversion to the first movement's expressive condition. But the immediate change of mind in bar 107 reveals 105–6 as an aberration, and the transformation of A minor into A major is secured at the Finale's threshold. As Appel explains, 'the transition's truly brilliant inspiration resides in the epigrammatic entwining [*epigrammatischen Verknüpfung*] of reminiscence on the one hand and anticipation on the other': bars 103–4 point towards the Finale; bars 105–6 point back to the first movement.[2]

Ingenious as this transition is, Appel's focus on it leaves untouched the important question of how the Intermezzo relates to the first movement's slow episode. The *Phantasie*'s *allegro molto* coda apes the style of a finale but is hardly a fully worked-out form in its own right; but as we have seen, the *andante espressivo* is a self-contained miniature, and, moreover, one consciously conceived on the model of a precedent – Field's Concerto No. 7 – which incorporates its slow movement at the same formal juncture. In keeping with the observation of a 'concerto within a concerto', the Intermezzo confronts the problem of tautology directly: Op. 54 in effect has two slow movements. This fact complicates both our interpretation of Schumann's aspirations for the genre and the views of commentators characterising Op. 54 as a major contribution to the development of the 'symphonic' concerto. Although the first movement's motivic economy and strong preference for integrating soloist and orchestra invite symphonic comparison, the Intermezzo reproduces the *andante espressivo*'s association with the lyric character piece at the level of the movement cycle.

Pace Dahlhaus, Juan Martin Koch and others, all of this suggests that a rich understanding of the Intermezzo and rondo, and by extension of the entire Concerto, requires more than a decision about generic classification, about what kind of concerto we think Op. 54 is. Rather, we need to acknowledge the full range of stylistic features Schumann deploys, to determine how they are mediated and ultimately to establish a reading that grasps the

Concerto's formal, material and expressive trajectory as a narrative of this mediation. The transition into the Finale is a critical moment precisely because it brings two elements in this narrative – the lyric and the symphonic – into contact at the Finale's threshold.

The Intermezzo

Form and Formal Function

The Intermezzo is formally simple but elusive in its details. It is cast in a clear compound ternary form, explained in Table 4.1, in which both A and B sections are themselves ternary designs (A1, A2 and A1^1; and B1, B2 and B1^1). As Juan Martin Koch points out, the sections are not materially discrete because, as Example 4.1 shows, the melody of the B section is constructed out of a fragment of the A section. Specifically, the pianist's music in bars 6–8 is taken up, in free augmentation, by the cellos in bars 28–31, and this idea is pervasive until A returns in bar 68.

The music's local organisation is somewhat more evasive. Section A begins in the manner of a classical sentence – the anacrusis and first half of bar 1 supply a statement, to which bars 1–2 furnish a response, and the stepwise progression in bars 3–4 adds a continuation phrase – but the cadential material is profoundly unclassical. Bars 4–6 initially suggest the onset of a perfect authentic cadence (PAC) in F, but in the end produce an imperfect authentic cadence (IAC) in the relative minor, which is immediately answered by a PAC in the dominant (Example 4.2). Classical precedents for evaded or deceptive cadences provoking PACs are widespread, but usually the successful cadence revisits and completes its unsuccessful predecessor, deploying what Janet Schmalfeldt has called a 'one-more-time technique'.[3] In Schumann's ending, the material of the second cadence is unrelated to that of the first. Nevertheless, the two cadences are not separate events but are harmonically overlapped. From the perspective of bar 8, we might reasonably elide the progression in bars 5–6 with a larger cadential span, which treats the D minor chord in bar 6 as ii in the V:PAC that follows. Diachronically, we

Table 4.1 *Schumann, Op. 54/ii, form*

Bars:	1	9	17	29	45	53	68²	77	85
Form:	A			B			A¹		
	A1	A2 (contrasting middle)	A1¹	B1	B2 (contrasting middle)	B1¹	A1	A2 (contrasting middle)	A1¹ (dissolving)
Key:	F:I			V			I		→a:V/i

The Intermezzo

Example 4.1 Schumann, Op. 54/ii, derivation of B from A.

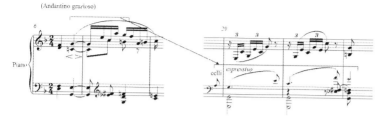

Example 4.2 Schumann, Op. 54/ii, A section, harmonic interpretations of bars 4–8.

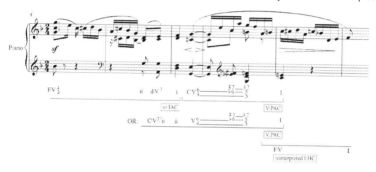

hear a D minor cadence as bars 5–6 pass by, which, retrospect-ively, we might fold into the PAC in C. This cadence is also rapidly qualified because the pianist's material in bar 8 returns us quickly to F, turning the cadence in bars 7–8 into what William Caplin calls a 'reinterpreted half cadence': a PAC in V reverts quickly to the tonic, and the arrival on V therefore sounds more like a half-cadence in the tonic than a full cadence in the dominant.[4]

A's contrasting middle section is also subtly adrift of classical convention. Typically, contrasting middle sections in classical ternary forms emphasise the dominant, either by standing on V or by returning to a tonic half-cadence at their end.[5] Schumann's A2 material, however, comprises a phrase and its varied repetition, which both end by asserting the tonic. In many ways, bars 9–17 audition more as post-cadential music of the kind normally

Example 4.3 Schumann, Op. 54/ii, A section, displacement dissonance in bars 20–5.

associated with a codetta, except to say that there has been no tonic cadence for them to follow, and they do not appear at the section's end. This technique can be described as a kind of formal *displacement*. Music we ordinarily hear at the end of a section or theme is dislodged from its customary habitat and made to perform a different function: here, codetta-like music is redeployed as a middle section.

The A section's internal reprise at bar 17 (A1¹ in Table 4.1) is also gently unorthodox, abandoning correspondence with bars 1–8 after two bars. Instead, Schumann uses the movement's distinctive step-wise head motive to construct a somewhat attenuated cadential phrase, which encounters a deceptive cadence in bar 24 before correcting to a successful PAC in bars 24–8. Anticipating some of the more extreme metrical distortions in the rondo, the downbeat emphasis shifts to the half-bar midway through bar 20, creating what Harald Krebs calls a –1 displacement dissonance: as Example 4.3 shows, derailing the alignment of notated and implied metre, the *sforzando* in the middle of bar 20 makes its second beat sound like the first beat of a new bar, but one that has arrived prematurely. This distortion persists for the rest of the A section. The deceptive V–vi in bar 24 elides with the start of the cadence's second attempt, which enters with the bar's second-beat D minor chord. And the cadence's ultimate tonic is placed midway through bar 28, such that the return to a notated downbeat emphasis at the B section's start mildly wrongfoots the music's metrical continuity.

The A¹ section, beginning at bar 68, largely reproduces the A section, with the crucial exception of the reprise, which fragments from bar 87 at the point corresponding to the displacement dissonance's introduction in bar 20. All of A's material after this point is abandoned except the sighing figure boxed in Example 4.3, which now alternates in falling sequence with a recall of the first movement's motive *y*, eventually settling on a half-cadence in A minor at bar 96, repeated two bars later, from which point the Intermezzo disintegrates without closure in readiness for the transition into the Finale.

B contrasts A and A^1 stylistically in that it is a fully fledged cantabile topic, resembling a nocturne in its melodic style and in the piano's accompanimental texture. Again, Schumann builds subtleties of formal construction into its design. B1 is a sentence: statement in bars 29–32; response in bars 33–6; continuation and cadence (a V:PAC) in bars 37–44. The contrasting middle (B2 in Table 4.1) is constructed as a sequence on the B1 section's head motive – model in bars 45–8, sequenced up a tone in bars 49–52 – but Schumann provides this progression with no clear harmonic terminus that differentiates the contrasting middle from the B1 reprise. Instead, the reprise begins at bar 53 and sounds initially like a further stage in the sequence, albeit one that does not follow the stepwise ascent pursued in bars 45–52 (the model is stated in G minor and sequenced in A minor; the reprise begins in C). In brief, contrasting middle and B1 reprise are elided, creating a kind of divisional overlap: from the perspective of bars 45–52, bars 53–6 are part of the progression initiated at the contrasting middle's start; from the perspective of bars 57–68, bars 53–6 belong to the reprise (the ambiguity is explained in Example 4.4). The sense of overlap is exacerbated by the bassline, which, from bar 53, reharmonises B1's returning first phrase over V^6/C rather than I, leaving the leading tone B adrift in the bass and requiring resolution, which is only forthcoming once the bass moves to C at the start of the response phrase in bar 57. From this point, B1 recurs verbatim, with some textural expansion, most notably the beautiful octave doubling of the final cadence's soprano line in violins 1 and 2, the effect of which is to complete a registral ascent of the B section's melody that ultimately spans four octaves from inception in bar 29 to completion in bar 67.

Example 4.4 Schumann, Op. 54/ii, end of B2 and reprise of B1.

Style and Genre

The movement's title itself raises questions: what does intermezzo mean in this context, and why is it applicable to this
movement? The term has operatic origins, being used in the
early eighteenth century to designate comic interludes ('intermezzi') inserted as *entr'actes* within larger, more serious stage
works. Schumann and Mendelssohn transferred it into instrumental genres, employing it to describe either character pieces

within larger cycles of miniatures (in Schumann's case) or the interior movements of sonata cycles (as in the third movement of Mendelssohn's String Quartet Op. 13). In both cases, the older, operatic implication of a lighter interlude between weighty movements is preserved, although to varying degrees. In the second movement of *Kreisleriana*, Op. 16, for example, Schumann inserts two intermezzi into a five-part design, which serve as energetic interludes contrasting the recall of a more reflective refrain. His *Intermezzi*, Op. 4, make the reinvention of the genre as a type of lyric character piece explicit. Schumann collects six pieces, some of which elide without a break, and all of which are constructed as multi-sectional forms, in which the sections are brief and self-contained. Opus 4 operates a conceit similar to that suggested by Chopin's re-conception of the prelude as a lyric genre. If preludes are improvisations in advance of more substantial pieces that never materialise, then the Op. 4 *Intermezzi* are *entr'actes* displaced from an imaginary larger work, into which they await insertion.

In Op. 54, the meaning of the Intermezzo's title is in one respect transparent, to the extent that the second movement evidently contrasts its far more substantial neighbours. Yet the invocation of the lyric character piece and relationship to the first movement suggest a more complex reading. In the first movement, as we have seen, the character piece is one element in a varied generic environment. The slow movement, in contrast, is a character piece writ large: in the Intermezzo, Schumann distils one feature of the first movement's style and allows it to define an entire movement. The second movement also has a particular relationship with the first movement's *andante espressivo* episode; and this returns us to Appel's perception that Op. 54 is 'a concerto within a concerto'. If the first movement *overstates* the role of the development's cantabile pre-core to the extent that it takes on the character of a slow movement, then the Intermezzo *understates* the role of an actual slow movement by styling it as an interlude, which is tonally open-ended and formally dependent on the Finale. In this respect, the *andante espressivo* and the Intermezzo are dialectically contrasted, and we might argue that the latter compensates for the former: a first-movement episode that aspires to the condition of a movement is balanced by a second movement that aspires to the condition of an episode.

Schumann's strategy is not unique. Beethoven composed slow movements in several genres, which are to varying degrees qualified as self-standing forms by the nature of their relationship with the Finale that follows. The habit of progressing from slow movement to finale without a break is especially common, and notably favoured in concerti. The slow movement of the 'Emperor' Concerto Op. 73 is the most oft-cited comparator because it too subsides to a moment of stasis in the Finale's key, in anticipation of an *attacca*. Similarly, the Larghetto of the Triple Concerto Op. 56 takes the form of an *arioso*, which, in direct analogy with Op. 73, comes to rest at a gestural low point in the Finale's key, after which the last movement's opening is texturally constructed out of the slow movement's melodic residues. The tonal strategy is the same in both pieces: a slow movement in ♭VI cedes to a finale in the tonic. The Larghetto of the Violin Concerto Op. 61 discloses a comparable, if less adventurous, strategy. Like Op. 73, it is organised as a set of free variations, which ends with a modulation towards the Finale's key; but here, the slow movement tonicises the subdominant, which means that the transition is less tonally abrupt. The slow movement of the Piano Concerto No. 4, Op. 58 is tonally closed but is in other respects more provisional than those of Opp. 73, 56 or 61 because it imitates an operatic recitative and therefore references no conventional generic form at all. Examples in other genres are readily apparent. An early instance tending more obviously towards the condition of an introduction appears in the String Quartet No. 6, Op. 18, the slow movement of which, entitled 'La Malinconia', gradually accrues a level of tonal ambiguity which it is left to the Finale to dispel. The slow movement of the 'Waldstein' Sonata Op. 53 is explicitly a slow introduction, being texturally fragmentary, tonally uncertain, formally ambiguous and titled 'Introduzione'. In the 'Waldstein', any form of self-standing slow movement has been entirely displaced by a prefix to the Finale.

And yet despite such obvious parallels, Schumann's slow movement differs from all these precedents in that, Op. 58's operatic resonances notwithstanding, Beethoven's provisional slow movements never step beyond the bounds of their genre in quite the same way. The importation of self-contained lyric elements into formal regions that are open-ended or unstable in classical precedents is a regular feature of Schumann's sonata-type works. One obvious parallel can be found in the Piano Sonata Op. 11, completed in 1835, which begins not with a rhythmically unstable and tonally provisional slow introduction of the sort common in classical sonatas – think, for instance, of the introduction to Beethoven's *Pathétique* Sonata Op. 13 – but with a self-contained, ternary form nocturne, which makes considerable rhetorical capital out of emphasising the stability of its tonic before the sonata-form *allegro vivace* begins. Having separated the introduction from the main sonata action, Schumann then works to reincorporate it, at two levels. First, the introduction's A section recurs in the first movement's development at bar 267, occasioning a sudden deceleration and draining away of the developmental momentum. Second, the introduction's B section supplies the main material of the slow movement. This music has additional lyric resonances because it began life as a setting of Justinus Kerner's poem 'Nicht im Thale' (*An Anna*), composed in 1828.[6] As in Op. 54, so also in Op. 11 a lyric *tendency* in the first movement blossoms into a lyric *form* in the slow movement: an Intermezzo in Op. 54; a song without words in Op. 11. The end of the Intermezzo in Op. 54 can, in turn, be interpreted as *a recession of the lyric*. Clearing the way for the Finale, the material of the character piece disintegrates, and quotations from the first movement remind us of the higher-level discourse between symphonism, virtuosity and lyricism, which is the outer movements' stylistic and aesthetic currency.

The Rondo Finale

Form and Tonality

The Finale is arguably Op. 54's most conventional movement. It ostensibly consists of a seven-part sonata rondo, rounded by a substantial coda, as described in Table 4.2. As Table 4.2 indicates, there are, however, regions of ambiguity which cloud the distinction between rondo and sonata. Primarily, the end of the

Table 4.2 *Schumann, Op. 54/iii, Finale*

Bars:	109	117	149	189	228²	359	391	485	497	529	569	608²	739	771	811
Form:	exposition					development			recapitulation					coda (rhetorical)	or: coda (structural)
	intro.	refrain	episode			refrain	episode		refrain	episode			refrain		
		A	TR	B	C	A (tutti)	C	RT	A	TR	B	C	A (tutti)		
Key:	I		→	V		V→		V/IV	IV	→	I				
Cadence:		I:PAC	V:HC MC	V:PAC	V:PAC				IV:PAC	I:HC MC	I:PAC	I:PAC		I:PAC	

The Rondo Finale

Example 4.5 Schumann, Op. 54/iii, end of exposition.

exposition, quoted in Example 4.5, plays off the expectation of a returning rondo refrain against the generic hallmarks of a solo exposition yielding to ritornello 2 in a type 5 sonata. An initial attempt at a dominant preparation for E major in bars 319–20 rapidly overshoots its harmonic goal and turns into a preparation of A major, after which the refrain (A in Table 4.3) reappears

127

conveyed by the tutti in bar 327 in the tonic.[7] The impression of a rondo reprise is then repealed with equal efficiency: A's head motive is immediately sequenced and V/V is re-established from bar 325, leading to a cadential trill over the dominant from bar 347, which duly resolves to E major in bar 359, where A enters with the tutti that is the exposition's true goal. The implication of a non-tonic rondo reprise is dispelled with similar haste: from bar 364 the theme fragments, giving way to a fugato at 367, which supplies the tutti's remaining material.

The music thereby implies three putative formal events – tonic A reprise, non-tonic A reprise and solo exposition–ritornello becoming development – in quick succession. In the recapitulation, the same sequence of events unfolds transposed into the tonic. This time, however, Schumann converts the tonic reprise of A, which in the exposition had dissolved into development, into a fully fledged rondo reprise, beginning in bar 739. Exposition and recapitulation are dialectically contrasted in this respect: the exposition's end sets up and confounds the expectation of a rondo refrain; the recapitulation's end confounds correspondence with the exposition by ultimately foregrounding a rondo refrain.

The Finale's form discloses other subtleties. The movement's central section might legitimately be labelled as a second episode or C because it introduces new material from bar 391, which pervades this section until echoes of the A theme return from bar 485, heralding the retransition. But the C material, although distinctive, is weakly thematic in its presentation. It has little of the form-functional stability or self-containment we associate with unambiguous C sections in classical rondos. A four-bar basic idea, stated in bars 391–4, is immediately repeated, and this whole eight-bar phrase is then sequenced up a tone and quickly fragmented towards the arrival in B flat major at bar 413, after which the whole section as far as the retransition is developmental. Again, Schumann intermingles sonata and rondo: the C section consists of new material, and consequently reinforces the perception of a rondo; but it is also substantially developmental, to which extent it defers to sonata form.

The rondo's formal ambiguities are abetted by its tonal scheme, summarised as far as the end of the recapitulation in Example 4.6.

Example 4.6 Schumann, Op. 54/iii, bass diagram (excluding coda).

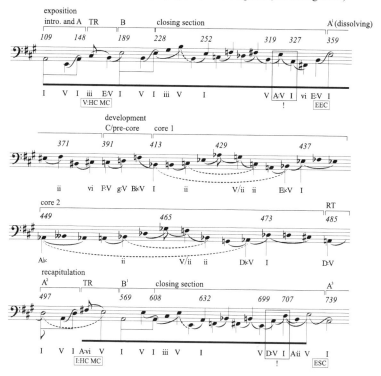

On the largest scale, Schumann revisits a strategy found in some classical sonata forms and repurposed in several movements by Schubert, which is the non-tonic recapitulation. The exposition progresses from A major to E major; the recapitulation begins in D major and the exposition's literal transposition ultimately returns us to A major, achieved with the return of the B theme from bar 569. The strategy is, however, more subtle than this because, as we have seen in the exposition, each tonally decisive return of the refrain is preceded by a false reprise, which anticipates the wrong key. In the recapitulation, the refrain returns in D from bar 707, prefiguring the true reprise, in A major, from bar 739. The retransition at the C section's end mobilises a similar idea: the head motive of A reappears in A major from bar 485, but this has become a dominant by bar 494, and the recapitulation-proper gets underway in D at 497.

The feint towards D in bar 707 carries an additional implication, which further complicates the picture. The impression is momentarily given at bar 707 that the recapitulation will be framed by D major, which means that, fleetingly, we are tempted to hear D as the movement's true goal and therefore to reconsider the whole design as a progressive tonal scheme, which begins in one key but is destined to end in another, the identity of which is signalled from the start of the recapitulation. When A^3 arrives in A major at bar 739, it not only restores D's true function as IV but also, finally, allows us to hear a false reprise as part of a process that secures the tonic. The uncertainties over the Finale's formal identity are imbricated with these tonal ambiguities. The clinching of A major at bar 739 is also the consolidation of rondo as the dominant formal paradigm, in effect compensating for the abortive reprise at A^1 and conclusively asserting rondo over sonata.

As Example 4.6 reveals, the development contrasts all of this by elaborating a Neapolitan complex: the C section enters over V of F in bar 391 (♭VI in relation to the tonic), but this turns out to be the gateway to a range of keys centred on B flat (♭II), which is reached at the start of the development core in bar 413. Conceived as a very large, twenty-four-bar model and its sequential transposition, the core tends increasingly towards extreme flat-side relations by pursuing a descending fifth progression, arriving a tritone away from the tonic in E flat at bar 437, then A flat major in bar 449, where the second rotation of the model begins, and finally D flat major in bar 473. Schumann's path to the recapitulation from this point is bold to say the least. In bars 475–84, the music traverses an enharmonic seam, which converts D flat into C sharp. The notation signifies a kind of enharmonic overlap here: the strings remain notated in D flat until bar 478; the piano converts D flat into C sharp major in bar 476. Schumann then drops directly onto A in bar 485 without mediation, exploiting a feature of what Richard Cohn calls a hexatonic co-cycle – that is, a motion between two major-third-related major triads – and this, in turn, is converted into V of D in preparation for the recapitulation.[8]

The whole impressive design is capped with a lengthy coda, which effectively behaves as a second development section to the extent that it explores the interaction of the A and C themes and consequently mingles ideas that are hitherto discrete. The coda immediately discloses an ambiguity because, as indicated in Table 4.2, its rhetorical and structural starting points appear at different locations. Rhetorically, we can hear the coda's start with the solo entry at bar 771, underscored by the *brillante* topic that is characteristic of virtuoso codas. Yet although the A theme's periodic form has rhetorically run its course by bar 770, Schumann withholds a PAC to round it off, instead undercutting the resolution of V by turning A major into V/IV in bar 770, progressing to IV in bar 771 and rapidly reinterpreting this as VI in F sharp minor, the dominant of which is introduced in bar 772. These delaying tactics are maintained until bars 807–11, where the soloist finally engineers a decisive tonic PAC. The result is a divisional overlap: rhetorically, the coda begins at bar 771; structurally, it begins at bar 811, once the huge expansion of the cadential progression initiated at 771 has completed.

Formal Function, Topical Discourse and Metrical Dissonance

Schumann's habit of writing themes that are clear in outline but complex in their details persists in the Finale. The A theme, given in Example 4.7, offers a particularly subtle instance. It is cast as a large period – antecedent in bars 117–32; consequent in bars 133–48 – prefaced by an eight-bar in-tempo introduction. The theme is ostensibly classical in terms of its phrase endings: the antecedent ends with a half-cadence, the consequent with a PAC. The interior design of both phrases is much harder to classify. The antecedent begins with a four-bar basic idea, bars 117–20, which becomes the movement's distinctive head motive and is followed by a contrasting idea from bar 121, which appears to conclude with a PAC in iii two bars later. This, however, is not the antecedent's ending, as we might expect in a classical period, but its midpoint. Bars 124–7 sequence bars 120–3 down a tone, a turn of events that causes us retrospectively to group bars 120–3 with 124–7 rather than with the basic idea: it now seems that the sequence of events thus far is basic idea–continuation (model+sequence). As a result,

Example 4.7 Schumann, Op. 54/iii, A theme, formal analysis.

we also need to rethink the harmony of these bars. Because bars
120–3 have been sequenced, we no longer perceive them to have
a cadential *function*, only cadential *content*: that is, their harmony
has the hallmarks of a cadence but the music does not perform
a cadential role in the theme's construction.[9] That task is now
taken by bars 128–31, which conclude the antecedent with what

Janet Schmalfeldt calls a 'nineteenth-century half cadence', meaning a half-cadence in which the ultimate dominant is coloured by its seventh.[10] The final bar of the theme serves as a voice-leading link to the consequent, incorporating a passing B sharp by way of a conjunct chromatic ascent to the basic idea's return.

The antecedent's various formal complexities generate ambiguities at the level of hypermetre: the grouping of bars within the theme can be interpreted in multiple ways. As indicated by the numbers above the stave in Example 4.7, the theme begins by positing a four-bar phrase and a three-bar phrase – bars 117–20 and 121–3 – but this reading is challenged as soon as we hear the ensuing sequence because, although bar 124 sounds like the start of a phrase unit, it stands in direct analogy with bar 120, which we have already concluded is the end of the basic idea, not the start of the contrasting idea. From the perspective of bar 127, bar 120 has a double identity: it is both the last bar of the basic idea and the first bar of the model, which is about to be sequenced. In other words, the grouping of bars here could either be 4+3+4 or 3+4+4. These possibilities coexist; which reading we choose depends upon where we are in the theme. The looming sense of hypermetrical irregularity is not dispelled by the cadence. Schumann's decision to add the passing harmony in bar 132 means that the cadential phrase is five bars long. In all, the antecedent yields two possible readings, neither of which is hypermetrically stable: 4+3+4+5 or 3+4+4+5. Schumann's positioning of *sforzandi* in bars 120, 124 and 132 exacerbates this instability because it consistently emphasises the functionally problematic bars. The consequent reproduces all of this verbatim with the small but crucial difference that the cadential phrase is shortened by one bar, in order to facilitate the conversion of the antecedent's half-cadence into a PAC. The dominant seventh in bar 131 corresponds to the same harmony in bar 147, but the latter is resolved directly onto I in bar 148, creating a five-bar cadential phrase for the consequent, in which the antecedent's dominant extension is replaced by the PAC's tonic of resolution.

Many of these phrase-functional ambiguities pass by unnoticed thanks to the music's subtle interplay of topic and metre, a feature that is particularly marked in the Finale. Like the first movement, the

Example 4.8 Schumann, Op. 54/iii, hemiola in B theme.

Finale both references and reimagines the topical contrasts of the virtuoso concerto. And again, the movement's inter-thematic functions are sharply delineated by topic. The A theme is a boisterous $\frac{3}{4}$ dance, redolent of the waltz finale of *Carnaval* or the opening movements of the *Davidsbündlertänze* and the *Faschingschwank aus Wien*. The transition immediately foregrounds display, but unlike the A theme, it moves entirely in clear four-bar phrases. The B theme is more topically and metrically evasive, introducing characteristic elements of metrical dissonance, particularly hemiola, which subsequently become a characteristic feature of the Finale. As Example 4.8 reveals, the music famously projects a $\frac{3}{2}$ metre against the $\frac{3}{4}$ time signature, generating what Peter Kaminsky and Harald Krebs call a 'grouping dissonance', which persists for the entirety of the B theme's small-ternary design.[11]

Following the theme's closing PAC in bars 228–9, a lengthy closing section begins, which retrieves TR's *brillante* topic and immediately pits the $\frac{3}{2}$ music against its $\frac{3}{4}$ alternative in rapid succession. The metre ostensibly settles into $\frac{3}{4}$ between bars 244 and 252, but in 253 Schumann reverts to $\frac{3}{2}$, adding the additional twist of what Krebs would call a +1 displacement dissonance: as revealed in Example 4.9, the material's sounding downbeat is the second beat of bar 253, but the piano proceeds as if this were the first beat of a $\frac{3}{2}$ bar.[12] From this point to the end of the exposition, the contest between $\frac{3}{4}$ and $\frac{3}{2}$ unfolds in five stages. In bars 252 and 286, the pianist maintains the displaced $\frac{3}{2}$ music, but the orchestra persistently interjects with fragments of the B theme, thereby insinuating a non-displaced $\frac{3}{2}$. At bar 286 the soloist shifts to

Example 4.9 Schumann, Op. 54/iii, metrical counterpoint beginning in bar 252.

a +1-displaced $\frac{3}{4}$ metre, but again the orchestra hold firm to the downbeat, suggesting a non-displaced $\frac{3}{4}$ grounded in a variant of the A theme's head motive. The abrasion of displaced and non-displaced $\frac{3}{2}$ and $\frac{3}{4}$ is then replayed in bars 294–326. The false reprise of A in bar 327 restores $\frac{3}{4}$, aligned with the notated downbeat, an event for which Schumann prepares with a final metrical misalignment. In bars 322–6, the pianist maintains the +1-displaced $\frac{3}{2}$ but is obliged to break off at the second beat in bar 327 as soon as the orchestra asserts the refrain. Contrastingly, the strings in bars 323–6 implacably demarcate the notated bar, sustaining the underlying ii^7–V^7 progression in A in two groups of two bars. From here to the exposition's end, $\frac{3}{4}$ asserts control, with one final, passing nod to $\frac{3}{2}$ in bars 343–6 as the soloist approaches their cadential trill.

These metrical complexities are the principal means by which the B theme and closing section are differentiated from the other regions of the form: A, TR and C all hold to a largely uncontested $\frac{3}{4}$ metre, notwithstanding their formal, textural and hypermetrical variety; B, in contrast, introduces a zone of metrical uncertainty, which is only dispelled with the A theme's return.

Theme, Motive and Development

Another important respect in which the Finale differs from the first movement is in its treatment of theme and motive. The first movement concentrates on a small fund of ideas, which are collaboratively exploited to generate its theme groups and supply the exclusive content of the development and coda. The Finale is both more fecund and more straightforward in its coordination of motivic material and the form's outlines. The first movement's multiple functional transformations are not replicated; Schumann mostly allocates discrete material to A, TR and B, which is unambiguously associated with these regions of the form.

The burden of motivic continuity, where it occurs, falls primarily upon the A theme's basic idea, which I label a. Example 4.10 charts a's treatment across the movement. As we have seen, it first recurs at the exposition's close, at the feint towards A major in bar 327. Schumann explicitly separates a from the theme's contrasting idea, both at this point and again when a forms the left-hand material beneath the cadential trill in bars 347–54. As the tutti approaches, the pianist then fragments a: in bars 355–7, only the leaping dyad with which a ends is preserved. At the tutti's start, the confident installation of a in the manner of a rondo refrain paradoxically promotes the impression that the motive's fragmentation in bars 355–7 presages the A theme's full return. But again, Schumann abandons the promise of a complete reprise, having restated a, and in bars 363–6 once more reduces a to its terminal dyad. This precipitates a further stage of development in which a is treated as the subject of a fugato, the countersubject of which is the A theme's contrasting idea, which I label b in Example 4.10. The fugato's purpose is not only to combine a and b but also to make their invertibility explicit: in bars 375–8, for instance, a appears beneath b, whereas in bars 379–82, b appears beneath a. Yet again, the goal of this process is fragmentation. Having previously focused on detaching the end of a from the motive's main body, in bars 383–90 Schumann jettisons the dyad and concentrates on fragmenting a's remainder, the assertion of which in the first violins twice provokes a chain of imitations, which isolate a's central portion. The process acting on a ends at this point: bar

Example 4.10 Schumann, Op. 54/iii, treatment of motive 'a'.

391 initiates the C section by introducing new material. The treatment of *a* between bars 327 and 354 is recapitulated in transposition in bars 707–39. Crucially, the tutti that is released at bar 739 in the wake of the soloist's cadential trill now follows

through on the promise of a complete restatement of the refrain, which means that the goal of the fragmentation process in bars 734–9 is essentially different from that of bars 354–9: the tendency for *a* to fragment is now arrested and the A theme is allowed to unfold in its entirety, and moreover in the tonic.

In the coda, *a* is subjected to a final phase of development, also traced in Example 4.10. This begins at bar 811, at the point where the tonic PAC deferred from bar 739 is confirmed and the structural coda identified in Table 4.2 begins. The process initiated here draws *a* and the C section's primary idea into a dialogue around the textural core of the pianist's ongoing display episode. The distribution of this material is charted in Table 4.3. The coda's process devolves into eight stages, each defined by the nature of the material under development. Six of these stages concern either *a*, C or their combination; two make no use of these ideas, for which reason I have defined them as 'interludes' in Table 4.3. Motive *a* is treated in three novel ways, in stages 1, 3 and 5, respectively. It is first compressed: the variant appearing in bar 811 occupies two bars, not four. In stage 3, the rhythmic profile of *a*'s second bar emerges in the strings at bar 848, supporting the piano's spinning out of C. Finally, in stage 5, *a*'s final appearance in the movement consists of a model-sequence progression, in which *a* twice appears in stretto at the unison and at a bar's distance. At bar 899, *a* is superseded by a recall of the pianist's broken-octave texture first introduced in bars 335–46, where it is employed to initiate the dominant underpinning the exposition's closing cadential trill. The final stage of the coda – the codetta beginning at bar 943 – is concerned entirely with C material.

The B theme, in contrast, participates negligibly in the movement's thematic processes outside the boundaries of its own theme group and closing section. Beyond its presentation in bars 189–228, it is only subject to significant developmental treatment in the interior of the closing section, bars 254–85, where the strings accompany the soloist's display material with fragments of the B theme's hemiola rhythm. This is naturally replicated in transposition in the recapitulation (bars 634–65), but as a matter of formal correspondence rather than development as such. The contrast between *a*'s developmental variety and B's comparative

Table 4.3 *Finale, coda, motivic design*

Bars:	811	835	848	859	883	911	927	943
Stages:	1	2	3	4	5	6	7	8
'a':	'a' compressed	-	residue of 'a' (bar 2 rhythm)	interlude 1 (b. 771 display material returns)	'a' model-sequence and in stretto	interlude 2 (new waltz material)	-	-
C:	-	C	C fragmented		-		C re-emerges	C-based codetta

inactivity is an important factor characterising the Finale's form and differentiating it from the first movement. In the *Phantasie*, there is no material distinction between theme groups, only between the ways in which shared material performs different formal functions. In the Finale, the form is articulated both by a contrast of thematic character and by the developmental narratives Schumann spins from his themes.

Texture, Expression and Society

Finally, the rondo is also vital in steering the Concerto to its expressive terminus, thereby bringing to a conclusion the ongoing dialogue between virtuosity, lyricism and symphonism that is central to the work's historical, aesthetic and socio-political identity. The Finale, in effect, caps Schumann's conversation with the genre, not only in the sense that it posits answers to a set of generic propositions that are established in the first movement but also because it brings to a point of culmination a process of thinking about the piano concerto stretching back nearly twenty years.

One obvious way in which Op. 54's movement cycle departs from virtually all classical precedents is in the way it invokes the minor–major trajectory more commonly associated with the Beethovenian symphony. Mozart's and Beethoven's concerti in a minor key maintain the minor modality into their finales and only convert to the tonic major at the end or, in the case of Mozart's K. 491, remain in the tonic minor. Subsequent minor-key concerti sometimes switch mode at the finale's start: Field's Concerto No. 7, Kalkbrenner's Opp. 85 and 107, and Ries' Opp. 115 and 132 all do this, for example.[13] Concerti that either sustain the minor mode until the finale's coda or else never switch mode are, however, at least as common. Chopin's Op. 21, Hummel's Op. 89, Kalkbrenner's Op. 61 and Ries' Op. 177 all save their major-mode turn for the finale's coda; and Hummel's Op. 85, Moscheles' Opp. 58 and 93, and Ries' Op. 55 never convert to the major mode. Schumann's dramatisation of the modal conversion in the transition to the Finale is more meaningfully anticipated by Mendelssohn, whose Opp. 25 and 40 both make a point of locating the mode switch in the Finale's introduction, which moreover follows from the slow movement without a break. In other respects, however, Mendelssohn's strategy differs fundamentally from Schumann's because Mendelssohn's movement elisions compensate for his habit of truncating the outer-movement forms, whereas Schumann's modal drama is played out across a fully worked-out type 3 sonata and an expansive sonata rondo.

In this sense at least, Op. 54 owes more to Beethoven's Symphony No. 5 than to his Piano Concerto No. 5: the opening of the Finale dramatises the alignment of the movement's start with the mode switch in a pointedly symphonic way. Yet paradoxically, the Finale that ensues owes more to older concerted precedents than the first movement and in consequence makes fewer concessions to the symphony. The most obvious evidence for this is found in the three substantial tuttis that punctuate the form, which increasingly resemble fully fledged ritornelli. The fact that Schumann makes a point of approaching the tuttis with which the exposition and recapitulation end with trill cadences redolent of a type 5 sonata's closing-section display episode adds further to the impression that the Finale is, to an extent, compensating for the absence of a sonata–ritornello hybrid in the first movement by recovering some of its properties in the last movement. Again, Schumann's generic strategies are dialectical: a feint in the symphony's direction produces a form that more obviously resembles a concerto; an overtly symphonic gesture leads to a more recognisably concertante design.

As in the first movement, so also in the Finale, all of this speaks to the genre's sociology as well as its formal expectations. The sense of aesthetic community between soloist and orchestra posited in the first movement is maintained but with a different expressive purpose: the first movement achieves and then retracts a positive minor–major trajectory; the Finale attains the major key's 'victory' and then sustains it. The instrumental distribution of material, traced in Table 4.4, is again instructive. Schumann associates the functions of the sonata with very clearly profiled textural principles. On the largest scale, the movement is organised around a basic dichotomy, between an A theme, the textural articulation of which is variable, and a B theme, the instrumentation of which does not change under recapitulation. To begin with,

Table 4.4 *Schumann, Op. 54/iii, form and instrumentation*

Bars:	117	149	189	205	213	228	252	327	359
Form:	A	TR	B	CM	B1	closing section	C2	C3	A¹
			B1			C1			
Theme:	piano	piano	strings, winds	piano	strings, winds	tutti/piano alternation	piano (display)	tutti/piano alternation (A anticipated)	tutti
Accomp.:	strings, winds	strings	-	-	piano display		strings		

Bars:	391	413	485	497	529	569	585	593
Form:	C (development)			A²	TR	B	CM	B1¹
	pre-core	core	RT			B1		
Theme:	wind/piano alternation	piano diplay/strings alternate accomp. and C theme	winds/strings (A anticipated)	tutti, alternating with piano in antecedent	piano	strings, winds	piano	strings, winds
			piano display					piano display
Accomp.:	strings				strings	-	-	

Bars:	608	632	707	739	771	811	835
Form:	closing section	C2	C3	A³	coda		
	C1						
Theme:	tutti/piano alternation	piano (display)	tutti/piano alternation (A anticipated)	tutti	piano display	tutti/piano alternation	piano display/ winds and piano alternate
Accomp.:		strings			strings		

Bars:	859	883	911	927	943
Form:	coda (cont.)				
Theme:	piano display	strings/winds	piano display	piano display	tutti and piano
Accomp.:	strings/winds	piano display	strings/winds	strings/winds	

A is allocated to the pianist. Thereafter, Schumann explores two alternatives: A^1 and A^3 are given purely to the tutti but are differentiated, in that A^3 is complete and A^1 is not; and in A^2, the antecedent is played by the tutti, while in the consequent, the soloist leads and the tutti responds. The contrast of first and second themes is consequently a contrast between two models of how individual and collective should interact. The refrain is dynamic, positing that the same idea can be distributed in different ways, and no one mode of ownership prevails. The second theme is static, not only because it is recapitulated without textural variation but also because it posits an order in which the thematic idea is always ultimately owned by the orchestra rather than the pianist.

A second obvious feature of the Finale is the much more explicit foregrounding of solo display. This is immediately apparent in the transition, which makes an obvious nod to the virtuoso concerto in that the pianist's *brillante* material does not elaborate an abstracted process of thematic presentation or development, as it does in the *Phantasie*, but constitutes a new, self-contained idea, the display topic of which is the material's distinguishing characteristic. The Finale is essentially different from the first movement in this regard: whereas in the first movement Schumann never allows display to become an end in itself, the Finale gives display topics their independence at the first opportunity and only later integrates them into less extrovert modes of discourse. The shift towards a more blatantly flamboyant solo rhetoric is one expressive means by which the climax of the struggle–victory narrative is articulated: once A major has categorically replaced A minor, virtuosity is liberated from its thematic confinement and starts to play a more decisive formal role.

Table 4.4 shows that the uses of solo display in the Finale move fluently between the textural foreground and the accompanimental substrate, concomitantly bringing precedents in the virtuoso type 5 sonata more fully to the fore. In the B theme, the soloist's first turn to *brillante* figuration occurs in $B1^1$, where it accompanies the theme's resumption in the orchestra at bar 213 following the contrasting middle. Having made display the transition's principal rhetorical focus, it is now returned to a subordinate role. In line with type 5 precedent, the closing section then reverses these roles again: after the alternation of tutti and solo in bars 228–44, the pianist's ongoing *brillante* figuration now takes centre stage, a division of labour that persists until the A theme reappears at bar 327. Both the development and coda dismantle this larger-scale alternation, breaking it down into a fluid interchange between emphatic virtuosity, discrete accompaniment and passages of transit between these poles. This is especially clear at the start of the development core: the piano leads with extrovert, bravura gestures in bars 413–21, but immediately retreats to a supporting role in bars 422–9 while the strings spin out the C theme. The pianist then tentatively recovers the spotlight in bars 430–7, producing a return to the material of 413–21, which is then sequenced.

The Finale's re-engagement with virtuosity should be interpreted not as a simple regression to an older model but as a kind of sublation or overcoming in the dialectical sense: the first movement internalises virtuosity, rigorously subordinating it to thematic and formal processes; the second movement suspends virtuosity altogether in order to prioritise lyricism; and the Finale reinstalls virtuosity at a higher level, reimagining it in the wake of the first and second movement's generic innovations. Again, this can be read in socio-political as well as textural, formal and aesthetic terms. The abhorrence of virtuosity's narcissism, which Schumann expressed in his critical writings, compelled a kind of concerto first movement, which imagines the genre as aspiring to a form of collective responsibility, in which all participants serve an ideal of thematic transformation, deploying the concerto's inherited formal and textural means to this radical end. In the Finale, the pianist is reinstalled not only as a free individual but perhaps as *primus inter pares*: as an equal who is nevertheless allowed a primary voice.

Notes

1. Bernhard Appel, 'Die Überleitung vom 2. zum 3. Satz in Robert Schumanns Klavierkonzert Opus 54', 260, translation mine: 'Dadurch entsteht quasi ein formaler Pleonasmus: ein Konzert im Konzert.'

2. Ibid., 261, translation mine: 'Der wahrhaft geniale Einfall der Überleitung besteht in der epigrammatischen Verknüpfung von Reminiszenz einerseits und Antizipation andererseits.' See also Daverio, *Robert Schumann*, 314.

3. Janet Schmalfeldt, 'Cadential Processes: The Evaded Cadence and the "One-More-Time" Technique', *Journal of Musicological Research* 12 (1992): 1–52.

4. See William E. Caplin, *Analyzing Classical Form: An Approach for the Classroom* (New York: Oxford University Press, 2013), 90–2. Caplin specifically associates these progressions with antecedent phrase endings in classical periods.

5. This property of classical ternary forms is explored in Caplin, *Analyzing Classical Form*, 197: 'The phrase structure of the contrasting middle typically consists of: a *standing on the dominant*; a *continuation phrase* ending with an HC.'

6. On which subject see Daverio, *Robert Schumann*, 144.

7. Note that bar numbers for the Finale are continuous with those of the Intermezzo in all modern editions I have consulted. Bar 1 of the Finale is consequently bar 109 in the score. Throughout, I have maintained these bar numbers rather than converting them into numbers that are specific to the Finale.

8. Richard Cohn, 'Maximally Smooth Cycles, Hexatonic Systems and the Analysis of Late-Romantic Triadic Progressions', *Music Analysis* 15/1 (1996): 9–40.

9. On the distinction between cadential content and cadential function in Romantic music, see Caplin, 'Beyond the Classical Cadence', 8.

10. Janet Schmalfeldt, *In the Process of Becoming*, 202–3: a nineteenth-century half-cadence is 'a local form-defining arrival on the dominant that, unlike the typical goal of classical half cadences, includes its seventh'.

11. As Krebs describes it, this is a situation in which music projects 'at least two interpretive layers whose cardinalities are different and are not multiples/factors of each other'; see *Fantasy Pieces: Metrical Dissonance in the Music of Robert Schumann* (Oxford: Oxford University Press, 1999), 31. Krebs calls a hemiola a 'G3/2' dissonance, meaning a dissonance in which groupings of duple and triple cardinalities compete within the same metrical span. Writing in the guise of Schumann's alter-ego Florestan, Krebs describes this passage in Op. 54 as 'surely my most celebrated example of subliminal dissonance' (*Fantasy Pieces*, 47, and see also 91).

12. *Fantasy Pieces*, 33–8.

13. Chopin's Op. 11 makes its switch to E major in the second movement and remains in the tonic major for the Finale.

5

RECEPTION AND LEGACY

Early Performance History and Critical Reception

Although Schumann's Op. 54 certainly belongs to the select group of piano concerti that have remained in the repertoire since their completion, it is by no means the case that it found a home in all places with equal speed or ease. By way of illustration, Table 5.1 compares data about the work's performance history between 1845 and 1900, compiled from the archives of the Leipzig Gewandhaus, the Vienna Philharmonic and the New York Philharmonic, as three institutions that were founded prior to Op. 54's completion, noting both the date of performance and the soloist; Table 5.2 rearranges the data by decade.

Table 5.1 makes one point very clear: assuming that the programming policies of the Vienna Philharmonic and the New York Philharmonic are at all representative of their cities' musical tastes, Op. 54 enjoyed a position in Leipzig's musical life more or less from the time of its first performance, which was not replicated in Vienna or New York. This is evident in baldly numerical terms – thirty-five performances across a sixty-five-year period with the Gewandhaus, as opposed to eleven with the Vienna Philharmonic and sixteen with the New York Philharmonic – as well as in the distribution of performances by decade. As Table 5.2 reveals, the work's presence in Leipzig is consistent from 1850 onwards: there are no fewer than five performances per decade at the Gewandhaus, rising to a highpoint of nine in the 1880s. The Concerto's history with the Vienna Philharmonic begins in 1860, with Clara Schumann's performance; thereafter its presence is consistent but slender. New York offers a more positive picture, revealing a steady increase in the number of performances with the Philharmonic up to the 1890s,

Table 5.1 *Performances by the Leipzig Gewandhaus, Vienna Philharmonic and New York Philharmonic by date and soloist*

Leipzig Gewandhaus		Vienna Philharmonic		New York Philharmonic	
1840s					
Date	**Pianist**	**Date**	**Pianist**	**Date**	**Pianist**
1/1/1846	Clara Schumann	-	-	-	-
6/4/1848	Clara Schumann	-	-	-	-
1850s					
Date	**Pianist**	**Date**	**Pianist**	**Date**	**Pianist**
7/2/1850	Wilhelmina Clauss-Szavardy	-	-	-	-
29/11/1855	Georg Mertel	-	-	-	-
8/1/1857	Clara Schumann	-	-	-	-
4/2/1858	Alfred Jaëll	-	-	-	-
20/10/1859	Louise Hauffe	-	-	26/3/1859	Sebastian Mills

1860s

Date	Pianist	Date	Pianist	Date	Pianist
1/11/1860	Hans Seeling	9/4/1860	Clara Schumann	22/12/1860	Sebastian Mills
29/11/1860	Clara Schumann	-	-	-	-
6/11/1861	Alexander Dreyschock	-	-	-	-
13/11/1862	Edward Dannreuther	-	-	-	-
11/12/1862	Clara Schumann	-	-	-	-
20/10/1864	Alfred Jaëll	22/1/1865	Louise Hauffe	-	-
-	-	-	-	-	-
6/12/1866	Heinrich Ehrlich	-	-	-	-
31/10/1867	Wilhelmine Marstand	-	-	-	-
-	-	20/12/1868	Auguste Auspitz-Kolar	1/2/1868	Sebastian Mills

1870s

Date	Pianist	Date	Pianist	Date	Pianist
3/3/1870	Louise Hauffe	-	-	-	-
1/1/1871	Emma Brandes	3/12/1871	Sophie Menter	-	-
19/10/1871	Clara Schumann	-	-	2/3/1872	Anna Mehlig
-	-	-	-	-	-
-	-	22/3/1874	Ignaz Brüll	-	-

Date	Pianist	Date	Pianist	Date	Pianist
-	-	-	-	20/3/1875	Sebastian Mills
30/11/1876	Clara Schumann	7/1/1877	Louis Brassin	-	-
-	-	18/7/1877 (Salzburg Festival)	Ignaz Brüll	-	-
24/10/1878	Clara Schumann	-	-	-	-
-	-	-	-	8/2/1879	Leonie Hein

1880s

Date	Pianist	Date	Pianist	Date	Pianist
28/10/1880	Jeanne Becker	12/3/1880	Ernst Löwenberg	-	-
-	-	-	-	12/3/1881	Rafael Joseffy
11/1/1883	Theodor Leschetizky	-	-	7/4/1883	Rafael Joseffy
6/3/1884	Johannes Weidenbruch	23/3/1884	Clotilde Kleeberg	-	-
26/3/1885	Clara Schumann	-	-	-	-
29/10/1885	Franz Rummel	-	-	-	-
11/11/1886	Agnes Zimmermann	-	-	9/1/1886	Carl Faelton
10/11/1887	Margarethe Stern	-	-	-	-
7/3/1889	Clara Schumann	-	-	-	-
7/11/1889	Carl Reinecke	-	-	-	-

1890s

Date	Pianist	Date	Pianist	Date	Pianist
26/11/1891	Eugen D'Albert	-	-	11/4/1891	Adele Aus der Ohe
-	-	-	-	19/11/1891	Ignaz Paderewski
30/11/1893	Margarete Voretsch	15/1/1893	Ilona Eibenschütz	10/3/1893	Ignaz Paderewski
-	-	-	-	11/3/1893	Ignaz Paderewski
18/10/1894	Sophie Vom Jakimowsky	1/12/1895	Fanny Davies	-	-
-	-	-	-	-	-
11/2/1897	Ignaz Paderewski	-	-	-	-
17/2/1898	Anna Langenhan-Hirzel	-	-	3/2/1899	Adele Aus der Ohe
7/12/1899	Ella Pancera	-	-	4/2/1899	Adele Aus der Ohe
-	-	-	-	15/5/1899	Louis Kroll or Frances Brandt
-					
Total: 35		**Total: 11**		**Total: 16**	

Table 5.2 *Performances grouped by decade*

Date range	Leipzig Gewandhaus	Vienna Philharmonic	New York Philharmonic
1846–59	7	-	1 (1859)
1860–70	9	3	2
1871–80	5	5	3
1881–90	8	1	3
1891–1900	6	2	7

during which decade Op. 54's popularity rivalled that apparent in Leipzig.

Another factor differentiating Leipzig and New York from Vienna is the notable championship of individuals. This, unsurprisingly, is most strongly evident in Leipzig, where Clara performed the Concerto nine times with the Gewandhaus between its Leipzig premiere on 1 January 1846 and her last Gewandhaus performance of it on 7 March 1889. Her association with the work peaks in the 1870s, during which she supplied three of the five performances at the Gewandhaus in that decade. Clara is, moreover, one of only three pianists to play Op. 54 in two of Table 5.1's three locations, performing it with the Vienna Philharmonic on 9 April 1860; the other two are Louise Hauffe, with whom it was played twice with the Gewandhaus (in 1859 and 1870) and once with the Vienna Philharmonic (in 1865), and Ignaz Paderewski, with whom it crossed the Atlantic, from New York in 1893 to Leipzig in 1897. Other prominent champions include Sebastian Mills, who gave the Concerto's New York premiere and who, more than anyone else, was responsible for establishing it there between 1859 and 1880, and Adele Aus der Ohe, with whom it came to be associated in New York in the 1890s. The data for Vienna is more evenly distributed in this respect, with the exception of Ignaz Brüll, who is the only pianist to perform the work more than once with the Vienna Philharmonic in this period, most strikingly at the Inaugural Salzburg Festival in 1877.

A further significant point revealed by Table 5.1 is the prominent role women played in the Concerto's early performance history. Clara's part in this history, of which the data in Table 5.1 provides only a limited snapshot, is naturally of primary importance but is nonetheless one element of a larger picture. The majority of performances at the Gewandhaus – twenty-two out of thirty-five – were given by women, who moreover account for half of the Concerto's soloists in that city up to 1900. In addition to Clara, female advocates at the Gewandhaus included Wilhelmina Clauss-Szavardy, Louise Hauffe, Emma Brandes, Margarethe Stern, Agnes Zimmermann, Jeanne Becker, Wilhelmine Marstand, Margaret Voretsch, Sophie vom Jakimowsky, Anna Langehan-Hirzel and Ella Pancera. A similar picture emerges in Vienna: six of the eleven Viennese performance featured women as soloist. The data for New York is less striking in this respect – three of the nine pianists cited are female – but Adele Aus der Ohe's advocacy is nevertheless an important factor. In the absence of comparative data, which might, for example, uncover the extent to which works by other composers benefitted comparably from female advocacy, it is rash to attribute any exceptional status to Op. 54 in this regard, although the impact of Clara's championship cannot be underestimated.

Pedagogical networks associated with the Schumanns also played a role in the Concerto's dissemination. Sebastian Mills, for example, studied at the Leipzig Conservatoire before settling in New York in 1856, and Edward Dannreuther was a student in Leipzig from 1860, where he was a pupil of Moscheles. Fanny Davies, who performed the Concerto in Vienna on 1 December 1899, attended the Leipzig Conservatoire in 1882–3 and studied for an additional two years with Clara Schumann in Frankfurt; Ilona Eibenschütz was also a product of Clara's tutelage at the Frankfurt Hoch Conservatoire.[1] Other connections can also be made: Wilhelmina Clauss-Szavardy, for instance, taught Auguste Auspitz-Kolar in Paris, who, in 1868, gave Op. 54's third performance with the Vienna Philharmonic.

Opus 54's critical reception in Germany, Austria and Britain makes for an instructive comparison. In Germany, the Concerto was immediately well received and comprehended in ways that anticipate some of the key themes considered earlier in Chapters 2 to 4. In London, it provoked varying degrees of suspicion and incomprehension for at least a decade after its British premiere in 1856, reflecting a general critical hostility towards Schumann's music, which prevailed until the 1870s.

Perceptive thoughts about the work's formal and generic approach are abundant in reviews of the premiere, given as a private performance by Clara in Dresden on 4 December 1845. Attributing his keen interest in the piece to the scarcity of modern piano concerti, the critic of the *Dresdner Abendzeitung* made flattering comparison with Adolph Henselt's Concerto Op. 16, which Clara had recently performed:

> We were particularly interested in a new concerto for pianoforte by Robert Schumann, partly because this is a field that very few composers who now have so much to do with etudes etc. cultivate (and such a limitation is commendable, as it belongs to that work more than the ordinary superficiality of most of our virtuosos, only laboriously disguised with a bit of glittering tinsel) – and then, because here the involuntary comparison with the Henselt concerto performed a few days earlier by the same artist was presented, which of course from this composition by Schumann sank completely into nothingness. We openly admit that we haven't heard such an interesting pianoforte composition as this Concerto for a long time[.][2]

Shrewdly noting that it is 'more an instrumental fantasy with piano in concerto form … than a true concerto', the reviewer lavished praise on every aspect of Op. 54's construction, instrumentation and aesthetic:

> Beautifully invented, spirited, interesting motives; very effective and clean instrumentation; pleasant rounding of the form; cozy tenderness and intimacy next to energy and passionate power; knowledgeable use of effects without gimmickry; clarity and transparency next to effortless work; melodious and characteristic treatment of the piano next to so much brilliance and bravura that even the virtuoso can feel satisfied with it; artistic unity in idea and execution: where all this unites, there can be no doubt about the value of a composition.[3]

Above all, the article extolled the Concerto's expressive unity, proclaiming that the three movements 'are cast in one piece, springing from a poetic idea, and a piece of the history of a human heart could easily be written out of these tones!'. Writing in the

Allgemeine musikalische Zeitung under the pseudonym 'Wise', Julius Schladebach reached comparable conclusions:

We have every reason to regard this composition very highly and to add it to the best of the composer's, particularly since it also felicitously avoids the usual monotony of the genre and does full justice to the obbligato orchestral part, which is worked out with great love and care without detracting from the impression made by the piano performance, and because it preserves the independence of both parts in a combination of great beauty. Amid the countless ephemera which every week brings forth in the field of piano compositions, it is a veritable delight to encounter for once such a worthy accomplished work.[4]

Again, the integration of soloist and orchestra is stressed, along with Schumann's ingenuity in avoiding the genre's outworn conventions.

Other German-language commentators were of similar mind. Appraising Clara's rendition under Mendelssohn's baton in Leipzig on 7 January 1846, the critic of the *Allgemeine musikalische Zeitung* also stressed the work's aesthetic coherence and deviation from the genre's formal conventions:

Her husband's new pianoforte concerto is a beautifully felt, deeply thought-out and spirited work, which gives gratifying proof that Robert Schumann's excellent talent also turns, with rare luck, to the composition of brilliant solo pieces. So that the expression just used does not give rise to misinterpretations, however, we add: the concerto should not simply be classified in the series of 'soli' because, unlike the concertos of a certain period, it does not break down into solo and tutti sections, but in a symphonic way creates a tone painting in which the pianoforte plays the leading role. This change of colour, this grasping and mutual transfer of independence between orchestra and piano gives the piece a special charm and forms it into a beautiful, well-rounded whole.[5]

Schumann's ambition to collapse both the formal opposition of soloist and orchestra and their textural separation is once more perceptively identified, and the later habit of affiliating the work more closely with the symphony is also anticipated.

Having first performed the Concerto in Vienna in 1847, Clara returned with it in 1858, provoking a review from Eduard Hanslick, who reproached Viennese pianists for not having risen to its challenges: 'This Concerto, listed as "new" on the programme, is nonetheless the same one we heard in Vienna eleven years ago; Schumann conducted it at the time, Clara played the piano. The fact that no one has played it since then can at most be explained by its great difficulty, or by the even greater indolence of our pianists.'[6] For Hanslick, Op. 54 was one of Schumann's 'most mature' and 'most thoroughly worked-out compositions [*reifsten, ausgearbeitetsten Compositionen*]', produced during the happiest and most productive phase of his career. Hanslick's understanding of the first movement's form goes beyond the Dresden and Leipzig critics in that he picks up on its nascent two-dimensionality: 'A short "Allegro molto" closes the first movement, which in its sequence of moderate, rapid, slow and rapid movement is itself the condensed image of an entire concerto.'[7]

The early history of Op. 54's British reception is to a large extent the history of Clara Schumann's performances of it.[8] Concert tours of Britain constituted the largest fraction of Clara's overseas travel: between 1856 and 1888, she visited Britain on nineteen separate occasions, programming Op. 54 in 1856, 1865, 1868, 1869, 1870, 1877 and 1887, as one of a select group of concerti she performed regularly, which also included Beethoven's concerti nos. 3, 4 and 5, Mendelssohn's two concerti, Chopin's F minor Concerto Op. 21, and Mozart's D minor Concerto, K. 466.[9]

Contrasting German enthusiasm, British critics of the 1850s and 1860s viewed Schumann with marked suspicion. For some, he was a dangerous radical, allied with Wagner, whose music frequently strained comprehension. Responses to Clara's performances at the Philharmonic Society Concerts in 1856 consequently differentiated her impeccable playing from the Concerto's general incomprehensibility. A review of her first Philharmonic concert, published in the *Daily News* on 15 March, cited Op. 54 as the evening's 'most interesting feature', since it 'was the first time that one of [Robert's] greater works has been performed in public' in Britain.[10] Clara is praised as 'the most accomplished female pianist in Europe', who played the Concerto 'with all her heart and soul'. Yet despite an overall sense that this was 'a great and beautiful work', and particularly that the Intermezzo 'is lovely from beginning to end', the critic confessed that 'in the other movements we found much that we could neither understand nor enjoy'. Responding to the third concert in the series in May 1856, the critic of *The Standard* expressed open hostility, complaining that 'the music of this concerto bristles throughout with the conceits and eccentricities which belong so disagreeably to the new school now struggling for existence in Germany, and of which Wagner and Schumann are the principal upholders and illustrators'. He was particularly dismissive of what he regarded as Schumann's privileging of idiosyncrasy over coherence: 'It would be impossible to admire such oddities of thought and expression at first hearing, nor would further acquaintance be likely to conciliate the sympathies, the governing fact being but too apparent that the music is a mere mechanical manufacture, and disfigured by caprices of detail, without any other motive than that of being purposely fantastic.'[11]

Clara returned to London with Op. 54 in May 1865, but *The Standard*'s views had scarcely changed, its critic complaining that although they liked her playing 'infinitely', they liked the music 'not at all', hearing 'nothing in it to admire, nothing to surprise, nothing to please, nothing to gratify' and concluding that 'if Schumann's concerto in A minor be good music Beethoven's concerto in E flat is not music at all'.[12] *The Era*'s reviewer reached a similar conclusion: 'Not even the delicate execution and unaffected expression characteristic of Madame Schumann's performances can ever popularise the new school music, and in the minds of very many persons it is not desirable that the simple and tangible models of the past should be set on one side in favour of the perhaps clever obscurity of the German present.'[13]

Critical opinion in the London press began to shift in the late 1860s. Reviewing Clara's performance of February 1868 at the Crystal Palace, the *Daily News'* critic challenged prevailing opinion:

We have always held that the pianoforte works and songs of this composer are his best ... and among the former his Concerto is conspicuous. It is not to be depreciated because it is not so clear and regular in form as the concertos of Mozart, or so vast and profound in its independent waywardness as the great concertos of Beethoven. The force and originality of this work ... should be apparent to all who are not afflicted by a persistent determination to depreciate a composer who has been even more underrated by some than overrated by others.[14]

This view is amplified, and Schumann's posthumous struggle for recognition in Britain explained, in an unsigned article in the *Pall Mall Gazette* dated 30 November 1868. The author insists that Schumann 'has had to fight for every step towards public favour' because he cares 'less for the beauty of his work than for its faithfully reflecting certain trains of thought or emotional conditions', concluding that

the author of Schumann's four symphonies, of the pianoforte concerto in A minor, of the quintet in E flat, of 'Das Paradies und die Peri' and of much other of a like sort should be welcomed as one who speaks, because having something new to say. His speech may be strange, but that of itself is no reason for rejection or even doubt.[15]

This positive impetus gained further momentum in responses to Clara's next rendition of Op. 54, at the Crystal Palace on 20 February 1869, to which the critic of the *Morning Post* reacted with unqualified enthusiasm:

Full of new melodies and unusual harmonies, the concerto possesses beauty of no common order, none of which is lost when Madame Schumann exhibits it with a loving hand. The beauty is placed in a most favourable light, that admiration may be won even from those who are unable to appreciate the full extent of the grace, symmetry and harmony.[16]

By 1870, positive reactions were becoming commonplace. A *Morning Post* review of Clara's Crystal Palace performance on 5 March 1870 is typical, welcoming 'a work full of evidence of the superiority of the mind of the author, who is now beginning to take his proper rank in the art in which he worked so nobly'.[17] The *Pall Mall Gazette* is a little more guarded, but nonetheless optimistic, finding 'a good deal [that is] hard to understand' but also 'a good deal in it the beauty and charm of which increase with acquaintance'. Furthermore: 'As to the excellent manner of its scoring, and its effective and grateful, though extremely brilliant, passages for the piano, there can be scarcely two opinions.'[18]

The increasing security of Op. 54 in the British concert repertoire after 1870 is evidenced by the expanding range of pianists who programmed it. Contrasting Clara's lone championship up to 1870, the 1870s and 1880s saw performances in London by Oscar Beringer, Walter Bache, Anna Mehlig, Eugen D'Albert, Anton

Table 5.3 *Hallé orchestra performances by date*

Date	Pianist
3/12/1868	Sir Charles Hallé
11/11/1869	Sir Charles Hallé
27/10/1870	Sir Charles Hallé
8/2/1872	Sir Charles Hallé
6/3/1873	Sir Charles Hallé
14/1/1875	Sir Charles Hallé
8/3/1877	Sir Charles Hallé
20/11/1879	Sir Charles Hallé
4/1/1883	Sir Charles Hallé
20/11/1884	Agnes Zimmerman
1/11/1888	Sir Charles Hallé
26/12/1889	Sir Charles Hallé
29/10/1891	Sir Charles Hallé
7/2/1895	Ignace Paderewski
30/1/1896	Ilona Eibenschütz
3/12/1896	Mark Hambourg
9/2/1899	Leonard Borwick
18/1/1900	Ilona Eibenschütz
22/11/1900	Moritz Rosenthal

Rubinstein, Sophie Menter, Natalia Janotha, Fanny Frickenhaus and Fanny Davies.[19] Interest also proliferated beyond the capital. Table 5.3, for example, collates information for Manchester's Hallé Orchestra. The pattern is similar to London but is displaced by a decade: between 1868 and 1884, the work is advocated by one pianist, Sir Charles Hallé, after which the pool of artists begins to diversify. Overlaps with the information for Leipzig, Vienna and New York are also instructive. Paderewski is again present; and Agnes Zimmermann, who performed Op. 54 in Leipzig in 1886, was the first pianist after Charles Hallé to perform it in Manchester. Again, Clara's pupils are a notable presence: Fanny

Davies and Natalia Janotha in London; and Ilona Eibenschütz, whom the Hallé hosted twice, in 1896 and 1900.

Beyond 1900, Op. 54's position in the performing canon is perhaps best captured by its discography. Responding to a 2020 edition of BBC Radio 3's record-review programme 'Building a Library' devoted to Schumann's Concerto, an especially diligent listener assembled and posted a comprehensive list of recordings on the radio station's online listeners' forum, which I adapt and extend, with details of recording labels and years of release and recording added, in Appendix II.[20] The list comprises 155 recordings and is notable for its historical and geographical diversity. Pianists long associated with the work are predictably prominent: Martha Argerich, Sviatoslav Richter, Arturo Benedetti Michelangeli, Artur Rubinstein, Claudio Arrau, Alfred Brendel, Walter Gieseking and Annie Fischer all recorded it multiple times, and others who have only recorded it once, such as Maurizio Pollini, have nevertheless made it a regular feature of their concert programmes. The discography tracks back into the early history of recorded music – Alfred Cortot, Annie Fischer, Yves Nat, Dame Myra Hess, Wilhelm Backhaus, Artur Schnabel and Clara Haskill are all represented – and also betrays the recent influence of historically informed performance (Andreas Staier and Philippe Herreweghe's period-instrument Orchestre des Champs-Élysées, for example, and Alexander Melnikov with the Freiburger Barockorchester). The geographical diversity of the ensembles involved is also conspicuous, spanning across Europe and beyond: in addition to Austria, Germany, France, the Netherlands, Italy, Russia, Switzerland, Czechia, Hungary, Poland, Bulgaria, Slovenia, Denmark, Sweden, the USA and the UK, Israeli, Turkish and Ecuadorian orchestras are listed.

The sheer range of recordings in Appendix II signals that Op. 54 has, in the last one hundred years, acquired a meaning for musicians that long transcends the work's time and place of origin and its circumscribing political context. Abetted by twentieth-century technologies of mechanical and digital reproduction, the efforts of Clara Schumann to popularise the Concerto in the decades after her husband's death have succeeded beyond anything she could have imagined.

Compositional Legacy

The natural first port of call for any appraisal of Op. 54's compositional traces in subsequent repertoire is Brahms, whose concerti are often cited in this regard, for instance in Juan Martin Koch's study of the symphonic concerto, which counterpoints Schumann's Op. 54 with Brahms' Piano Concerto No. 2, Op. 83. And yet the formal solutions that Brahms favoured in both his piano concerti differ in key respects from those of Schumann. Above all, Brahms revitalised the type 5 sonata. This is only partly realised in the first movement of Op. 15, which begins with a very substantial ritornello but abandons the type 5 scheme as soon as the soloist enters; but it is much more clearly apparent in Op. 83, the first movement of which includes two large ritornelli, in keeping with the habits developed in the Violin Concerto and Double Concerto, both of which employ three ritornelli in their opening movements. Moreover, Brahms never took up the formal challenge laid down by the *Phantasie* of 1841, the nascent two-dimensionality of which plays no role in any of his concerti; neither did he ever compose intermezzi after Op. 54's precedent in the slow-movement position or elide slow movement and finale.

Debts to Schumann in the Germanic repertoire are more readily discovered in Xaver Scharwenka's Concerto No. 1, Op. 32 of 1876, popular in its time but now sunk in obscurity. Scharwenka's first movement, like Schumann's, is a type 3 sonata, the development of which begins with a slow episode. Scharwenka expands Schumann's precedent in two ways. First, Scharwenka's slow episode occupies the entire development, not just its pre-core. Second, this section *is* the work's slow movement; the interior movement is a scherzo, which is strongly redolent of Schumann's Finale, mingled stylistically with Chopin's Rondo *à la mazur*, Op. 5 and the finale of his Concerto Op. 21. Scharwenka here picks up the example of Field's Concerto No. 7 and brings it into contact with Litolff's idea of the *concerto symphonique* by exploiting the slow movement's displacement as an opportunity to introduce a scherzo, while ostensibly preserving the genre's three-movement scheme. The work is also densely cyclical: material introduced in the first-movement exposition reappears in the slow movement, and extensively in the finale, culminating in the movement's coda, which consists of a wholesale, explicit retrieval of the first movement's first theme.

Examples of Op. 54's influence are comparatively plentiful in the Scandinavian and Russian repertoire, apparent in the adoption, variation and expansion of the formal solutions for which Schumann advocated. Some instances are transparent and unmistakeable. Grieg's A minor Concerto, Op. 16 of 1868, is perhaps the most blatant example. The debt to Schumann is evident in the first movement's introduction, first theme and start of the transition. The music's formal and stylistic proclivities mimic Schumann at every stage: Grieg also begins with a brief, in this case five-bar, bravura flourish, released by an orchestral hammer blow and prefacing a lyrical first theme; like Schumann's, Grieg's first theme is periodic and divides its formal duties so that the orchestra conveys the antecedent and the soloist responds with the consequent; and completion of the consequent's perfect authentic cadence (PAC) also initiates a transition, which introduces characteristic virtuoso passagework. Rachmaninov's Piano Concerto No. 1, completed in 1891 and revised in 1917, follows the same paradigm, albeit with some variations. Rachmaninov expands the bravura preface by doubling its proportions: the opening brass fanfare recurs in bar 9 after the pianist's bravura incipit, in effect cleaving the preface into two parts; and a second orchestral hammer blow in bar 13 precipitates an extravagant arpeggiated flourish and half-cadence in widely spaced octaves and chords, which parallel the ending of Grieg's preface. Thereafter, Rachmaninov follows Schumann and Grieg closely: the first theme is periodic and allocates the antecedent to the orchestra and the consequent to the soloist; and the display episode follows on from a tonic PAC in bar 32.

Grieg and Rachmaninov imitate Schumann in other ways. Both adopt Schumann's decision to punctuate exposition and development with a single tutti of sufficient size that it almost recalls the R2 of a type 5 sonata in scale and expressive import

(Rachmaninov's tutti is notably expansive in both the 1891 and 1917 versions); and both compose substantial cadenzas between the recapitulation and the coda, which in effect serve as secondary development sections. In his later concerti, Rachmaninov moved away from Schumann's first-movement precedent in key respects, keeping the type 3 frame in his first movements but jettisoning the bravura preface–periodic theme model and the punctuating post-expositional tutti. In the Concerto No. 3 of 1909, Rachmaninov revisits Schumann's resuscitation of the cadenza and substantially expands its formal significance. The cadenza begins at the start of the retransition over V of D minor, in which respect Rachmaninov references the first movement of Tchaikovsky's Piano Concerto No. 2, the cadenza of which bisects development and recapitulation, and ultimately Mendelssohn's Violin Concerto. Rachmaninov's cadenza, however, outgrows this formal context. Its climax is a forceful tonic presentation of the first theme, which turns out to be its recapitulation. A first-theme-based transition then ensues, which folds in solos from the flute, clarinet and first horn, but these orchestral interjections are transient and lead to the second theme's reprise, now again within a cadenza, in E flat, in which key the recapitulation ends with a brief codetta. The return of the orchestra re-establishes D minor and recalls the first theme, although this is the movement's coda. In effect, Rachmaninov's cadenza bursts its formal frame and engulfs the entire recapitulation, producing what Hepokoski and Darcy might identify as a 'sonata failure' because the recapitulation's action ultimately favours a non-tonic key.[21] The trajectory of first-movement cadenza composition traceable from Schumann to Rachmaninov travels in precisely the opposite direction to that mapped out by the early nineteenth-century virtuoso concerto. Whereas the latter disposes of the cadenza altogether, the former incorporates it as a through-composed feature, mobilising it as a locus of development and ultimately expanding it to the dimensions of a large-scale formal event.

In Grieg's Op. 16 and Rachmaninov's Concerto No. 3, the analogy with Schumann extends beyond the first movement because in both works the slow movement and finale are elided.

Grieg's slow movement is also notably abbreviated, although, unlike Schumann, Grieg secures his adagio's key with a clear PAC before engineering the inter-movement transition. Rachmaninov is in one sense closer to Schumann because his slow movement is explicitly described as an intermezzo. On the other hand, Rachmaninov follows the precedent of Tchaikovsky's Concerto No. 1 by folding a scherzo episode into his slow movement, thereby enhancing the work's symphonic resonances but departing considerably from Schumann's lyric miniaturism. And Rachmaninov's transition tends towards bravura extroversion in its pianism and a monumentality of gesture, which further underscores symphonic aspirations.

Other Russian repertoire foregrounds different aspects of Schumann's practice. The first movement of Anton Rubinstein's Concerto No. 4 of 1864 amalgamates elements of Schumann's type 3 design with textural ideas transparently borrowed from Schumann's Introduction and Allegro Appassionato, Op. 92 (notably the start of the transition, which resembles the equivalent passage in Op. 92 to an extent that borders on plagiarism), while also betraying Mendelssohnian influences. Rubinstein, like Schumann, begins his Concerto with a bravura preface and a periodic first theme shared between orchestra and piano, but rearranges these components. The orchestra states the first theme's antecedent in bars 1–24, but its proportions are heavily distorted: a converging half-cadence is reached after eight bars, after which the music stands on the dominant for seventeen bars in preparation for the soloist's entry, which arrives in bar 25 with an extrovert, fourteen-bar bravura flourish. The pianist then picks up the first theme and supplies a consequent phrase, closing with a tonic PAC in bars 53–4. Rubinstein's strategy for the cadenza also invokes Schumann. Like Schumann, Rubinstein releases his soloist into the cadenza by disrupting the music's flow with a rhetorically marked arpeggiation of ♭VI (the two passages are compared in Example 5.1). Rubinstein is more adventurous than Schumann because his second theme is itself recapitulated in ♭VI (B flat major), which means that the cadenza intervenes on G flat, a diminished fourth away from the tonic, D minor. Moreover,

Example 5.1 Comparison of Schumann, Op. 54/i and Rubinstein, Op. 70/i, cadenza openings.

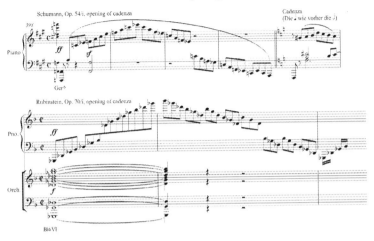

Schumann quickly resolves his ♭VI as an augmented sixth in the cadenza's early stages; but Rubinstein's persists in G flat, which means that his cadenza has the task of returning the music to D minor, which is achieved with a dramatic final tutti assertion of the first theme in advance of the coda.[22]

Tchaikovsky favoured the type 3 sonata in all three of his first movements, and, like Schumann, employs one centrally positioned tutti, immediately following the exposition in the concerti Nos. 1 and 3, and midway through the development in the Concerto No. 2. Tchaikovsky also adopted Schumann's cadenza strategy in his Concerto No. 1 but shifted the cadenza into the re-transitional position in No. 2 and enlarged it to encompass much of the development section in No. 3. Schumann's fingerprints also surface at the inter-thematic level in Tchaikovsky's concerti, especially in the first-movement closing sections of Nos. 1 and 2, which merge thematic presentation and display-episode rhetoric in ways strongly redolent of Op. 54. Example 5.2 quotes the exposition's second-theme B1 section and the start of its reprise in the first movement of Tchaikovsky's Concerto No. 1. Tchaikovsky follows Schumann's lead in transferring the music's

Example 5.2 Tchaikovsky, Op. 23/i, second theme B1 section antecedent and start of B1 reprise.

brillante display to the texture's interior, where it supports the B1 reprise. The second theme and closing section are also functionally complex in ways that resonate with Op. 54, even though the details are different; Table 5.4 elucidates their design. Tchaikovsky's second theme begins as a large period in which the antecedent is taken by the orchestra and the consequent by the pianist. At bar 204, this is revealed as the first section of a ternary design (B1) because a new idea (B2) begins at this point in a contrasting key, after which B1 returns at bar 218, which is where the display characteristics in Example 5.2 intervene. Tchaikovsky's theme is tonally evasive in a way that adds to its form-functional complexity. It begins in the tonic and insinuates A flat via a half-cadence at the antecedent's close, but the consequent initially returns to B flat minor before cadencing with a PAC in C minor. The implication of A flat is then picked up by the contrasting middle, which is rooted to an A flat pedal for

Table 5.4 *Tchaikovsky, Op. 23/i, second theme and closing section, formal analysis*

Bars:	184	192	204²	218	226	267
Form:	B1		B2	B1¹⇒C		
	antecedent	consequent	contrasting middle	antecedent	consequent	codetta
Key and cadence:	i→VII:HC	i→ii:PAC	VII→V/i	i→VII:HC	i→ii:PAC (expanded)	VII

much of its duration, but the reprise simply returns to the theme's tonic opening. Eventually, $B1^1$ expands the consequent's C minor PAC, tonicising that key with high drama in bars 240–66 in the manner of a display-episode closing section. Yet Tchaikovsky serves up a twist, appending a codetta, which returns to the contrasting middle's material and key, rounding off the exposition in A flat and thereby securing a kind of tonally bivalent ending. Altogether, Tchaikovsky engineers a divisional overlap on an impressive scale: closing-section rhetoric is introduced from bar 218, while the second theme is still underway; and the closing section proper, which follows the decisive C minor structural cadence (from bar 267), has nothing to do with that cadence's key.

Schumann's innovations also made their mark in western Europe and beyond. In France, no composer did more to sustain the genre in the second half of the nineteenth century than Saint-Saëns. Although the influence of Mendelssohn and Liszt is plain to see in Saint-Saëns' five concerti, there are regular conceptual and stylistic nods in Schumann's direction. The first movement of his Concerto No. 1 in D major (1858) resonates with Op. 54 in several respects. Saint-Saëns conceives a type 3 sonata prefaced with a brief slow introduction adumbrating the first theme. Saint-Saëns' design goes beyond Schumann in its dissolution of the type 5 sonata, in that, with the possible exception of the orchestra's majority presentation of the first theme, it entirely does away with punctuating orchestral tuttis. Saint-Saëns also folds virtuosity and display into the textural interior of his exposition's thematic discourse. The whole of his transition and second-theme audition as a continuous display episode: the pianist's *brillante* figuration, initiated at bar 57 with the start of the transition, is maintained when the second theme commences in bar 84 without any suggestion of a medial caesura. As for Schumann, so also for Saint-Saëns, the thematic substance of the form is conveyed largely by the orchestra, which the soloist's display material augments and elaborates.

Of Saint-Saëns' subsequent concerti, Nos. 2, 3 and 5 maintain a preference for type 3 first movements, which build on the textural habits introduced in his Concerto No. 1 (the Concerto No. 4 is a fully fledged two-dimensional form, and as such perhaps owes more to Liszt's Concerto No. 2 than Schumann's Op. 54). His most substantial type 3 form appears in the first movement of the Concerto No. 3 in E flat, Op. 29 of 1869. Saint-Saëns again composes a slow introduction, which adumbrates the *allegro*'s main theme. His exposition is radical in two respects. First, his second group is conceived as a slow episode in the manner of the *andante espressivo* of Schumann's *Phantasie*, which is poised over the dominant of D, suggesting a secondary key area a semitone away from the tonic. Second, the entirety of the closing section is occupied by the cadenza, which reintroduces the first theme while sustaining an orientation around V of D. The tonic that this long dominant implies is, however, withheld at the exposition's end: the tutti entering at rehearsal letter D resolves the prior A dominant 7th deceptively to B flat major, and Saint-Saëns then proceeds directly to the development, as if the dominant of E flat had been the exposition's secondary key all along.

In Britain, Schumann's influence is especially obvious in Charles Villiers Stanford's Piano Concerto No. 2, Op. 126 in C minor of 1916. The first movement's type 3 design employs Schumann's by now familiar single, post-expositional tutti, which moreover cedes, at the start of the development, to a nocturne episode, quoted in Example 5.3, which patently invokes Schumann's *andante espressivo*. Stanford's homage is textural and tonal as well as topical and formal. Stanford's nocturne, like Schumann's, is cast initially as a dialogue between piano and clarinet, supported, in this case, by a solo cello, to which the remaining string group is gradually added. Stanford also conceives his nocturne as a point of maximum tonal distance from the first theme: here, the relative major attained at the exposition's end is displaced by G flat major, thereby positioning the development pre-core in tritonal opposition to the tonic. Ingeniously, Stanford underwrites the tonal logic of this remote modulation by situating it within a system of octatonic key relations. The progression underpinning the exposition and development pre-core describes the ascending minor-third arpeggiation C–E flat–G flat. Stanford then recapitulates the first theme in C major rather than C minor and exploits this modal mixture to reprise the second theme initially in A minor, only working his way back to C minor

Example 5.3 Stanford, Op. 126/i, nocturne episode at start of development.

for the movement's coda, which means that, by the end, the music has passed through the complete division of the octave by equal minor thirds: C minor–E flat–G flat–A minor–C minor.

In the USA, works by Amy Beach and Edward MacDowell add, in distinctive ways, to the genealogy of Schumann's Concerto.

Beach's Concerto in C sharp minor, Op. 45, composed in 1899, is symphonic in Litolff's sense that it expands to incorporate a second-movement scherzo. But her first movement, like Schumann's, is a type 3 sonata, and resembles Grieg, Tchaikovsky, Rachmaninov and Stanford in locating its principal tutti between exposition and development. Beach also conceives her first theme and transition as a transplantation of the virtuoso type 5's bravura–nocturne–*brillante* topical succession into a type 3 exposition, albeit in a more extrovert manner than Schumann. The idea of restoring the cadenza prior to the coda is also adopted: Beach's cadenza rivals that of Grieg's Op. 16 and Rachmaninov's Concerto No. 1 in substance and virtuosity. MacDowell's Concerto No. 2 in D minor Op. 23 (1885) is comparably symphonic in that its first movement is a type 3 sonata and its second movement is a scherzo. MacDowell's Concerto effectively contains two slow movements, which means that it confronts a problem of pleonasm at the level of the movement cycle that echoes Schumann's Concerto, although in MacDowell's case without the implication of a two-dimensional form. His first movement is a *larghetto*, which despite moments of drama and bravura owes much to the lyric character piece; and in place of a fully fledged interior slow movement, MacDowell writes a slow introduction to the Finale, which gestures to Schumann in its recall of the first movement as the last movement approaches.

Conclusions: Schumann's Piano Concerto and Our Time

In 1828, the eighteen-year-old Schumann composed an essay on the philosophy of artistic creativity entitled 'Über Genial-, Knill-, Original- und andre itäten'. The title is not easy to translate; John Daverio renders it as 'On Genial-, Insobr-, Original- and other i(e) ties'. Its wordplay seeks to capture the diverse uses of the German suffix '-ität', which converts adjectives into feminine nouns. Schumann focused on three such nouns – ingeniousness (*Genialität* in Daverio's translation), insobriety (*Knillität*) and originality (*Originalität*) – as central for any appreciation of artistic genius, and on *Genialität* in particular as a vital ingredient of the highest forms of art. For Schumann, *Genialität* was above all the capacity to resolve antitheses: he notes, for instance, 'the union of the sentimental and the humorous' in the writings of Goethe and the music of Beethoven and Schubert. Crucially, *Genialität* is not a purely innate capacity but is in Schumann's view acquired through 'self-formation': that is, through the process of cultural education ordinarily defined by the abstract noun *Bildung*.

The concepts of *Genialität* and *Bildung* together apostrophise the view of Schumann's Piano Concerto developed in this book. Readings of Op. 54 miss the mark if they try to position it on one side of the aesthetic debates between virtuosity, lyricism and symphonism. Evidence of all three can be readily identified: the first movement's thematic economy and its rejection of the type 5 sonata point towards symphonism; the topical hallmarks of virtuosity are abundant in the outer movements; and the idioms of the character piece are easy to discern in the first movement and intermezzo. Schumann's ambitions are synthetic rather than partisan: he is concerned to synthesise the genre's diverse ingredients in a work that is more than the sum of these parts, not simply to replace the virtuoso concerto with a symphonic alternative or, as Tovey argues, to 'solve' the problems bequeathed by the classical concerto by rejecting its models altogether. In short, Op. 54 exemplifies Schumann's propensity for *Genialität*: the meaningful synthesis of constitutive oppositions. Simultaneously, the work's overarching narrative – which tracks the progress of the soloist-as-protagonist from collaborative but ultimately tragic circumstances in the first movement to a celebration of autonomy amidst the orchestral collective in the Finale – offers a compelling allegory of *Bildung* in microcosm, which is political as well as aesthetic: Schumann appropriates the concerto as a medium for the representation of an ideal polity.

Viewed from the present, the idealism that Schumann's Concerto instantiates might seem at best naïve, at worst vulnerable to postmodern forms of ideology critique, especially decolonisation, which sometimes construes Western art music as an avatar of European imperialism and argues for restricting its musicological and curricular presence on the dual grounds of its past imperialist affiliations and its apparent function as a colonising force in our own time.[23] The relevance of Schumann's music in the present is additionally threatened by the seemingly terminal decline of the tradition to which he contributed, which has prompted commentators to prophesy the imminent demise of Western art music and its sustaining modes of musical literacy as meaningful features of our cultural landscape.[24]

In the midst of all this, it is hard to be optimistic about Op. 54's prospects in the twenty-first century. As we have seen, comprehending Schumann's subtle dialogue with the genre and the solutions to its dilemmas he conceived for Op. 54 requires us not only to excavate his concept of the concerto but also to re-engage with a repertoire which he regarded as self-evidently important, but which has since been largely lost to history. Although recent interest in the recovery of music by marginalised nineteenth-century composers – particularly women and composers of colour – is welcome, many works that are central to Op. 54's genesis remain invisible to music theory and consequently do not inform mainstream theoretical models. Moreover, if the forms of musical literacy that are essential to both the production and comprehension of Western art music dwindle away in the present, then the intellectual tools required to understand Schumann's Concerto, or indeed any of the music in the traditions to which he contributed, will become increasingly rare commodities. Perhaps we can soon expect a time when, as Richard Taruskin speculates, 'musical literacy, like knowledge of ancient scripts, [will become] superfluous to all but scholars'.[25] That superfluity does not bode well for our capacity to appreciate Schumann's music.

That this work, and the art it represents, should be preserved in our aesthetic, scholarly and intellectual lives is in one sense compelled by the rich and detailed understanding of history it enables. Much critical ink has lately been spilled over the complicity of Western art music with European imperialism; but even cursory appraisal of the historical circumstances that gave rise to Op. 54 reveals a level of cultural granularity which proponents of decolonisation fail to acknowledge. As Chapter 3 made clear, the Saxony into which Schumann was born engendered a political identity, the complexity of which thwarts any attempt to define Western art music in terms of an affiliation with some generalised notion of imperialism. Properly speaking, there is no German colonialism in Schumann's lifetime, or indeed any unified German polity before 1871. Schumann's cultural politics embody a kind of regionalism which has little in common with the discourses of imperialist exceptionalism that germinated in Britain and France at the turn of the nineteenth century. Schumann is, of course, a German composer; but the Germany of Schumann's imagination is a cultural and aesthetic ideal, not a constitutive political entity.

Yet if Op. 54 reminds us of the folly of essentialising history, then it is also worth remembering that art often outlives the circumstances of its production precisely because it has more to offer the world than the residues of its historical context. As we have seen, Schumann's Piano Concerto is not simply a passive reflection of its time but seeks to give musical voice to a species of cultural-political critique, which is radical because it imagines a better world, not an existing one. All concerti are, in one sense, allegories of their social order, but Schumann's Op. 54 is unique among early Romantic concerti in the democracy of its solo–orchestral interactions. At the end, the pianist emerges as an individual whose relationship with the collective is more profoundly collaborative and consensual than that evident in any of the concerti in Schumann's critical purview. And here is one of many good reasons to treasure this work: because in Schumann's humane and intelligent art, we find a better version of ourselves.

Notes

1. On Clara Schumann's tuition of Ilona Eibenschütz, see Reich, *Clara Schumann*, 283–5. An overview of Clara's pupils is also given in Therese Ellsworth, 'Women Soloists and the Piano Concerto in Nineteenth-Century London', in Therese Ellsworth and Susan Wollenberg, eds., *The Piano in Nineteenth-Century British Culture: Instruments, Performers and Repertoire* (Aldershot: Ashgate, 2007), 21–49, at 45.
2. 'Vorzugsweise interessierte uns ein neues Konzert für Pianoforte von Robert Schumann, einmal weil das ein Feld ist, das die wenigsten Komponisten, die jetzt so viel mit Etuden usw zu tun haben, anbauen (und solche Beschränkung ist lobenswert, denn es gehört zu jenen Arbeit mehr als die gewöhnliche, mit etwas glänzendem Flitter mühsam nur verhüllte Oberflächlichkeit unserer meisten Virtuosen) – und dan, weil sich hier unwillkürlich der vergleich

mit dem wenige Tage zuvor von derselben Künstlerin vorgetra-
genen Hentseltschen Konzerte darbot, das freilich von dieser
Komposition Schumanns völlig in das Nichts versank. Wir geste-
hen offen, seit langem nicht so interessante Pianofortekomposition
gehört zu haben als dieses Konzert[.]' *Dresdner Abendzeitung* 103
(25 December 1845): 1130–2, at 1131, col. 1. See also Gerstmeier,
Robert Schumann: Klavierkonzert a-Moll, Op. 54, 39–40, translation mine.

3. 'Schön erfundene, geistreich durchgeführte, interessante Motive,
sehr wirksame und saubere Instrumentierung, wohlteunde
Abrundung der Form; gemütliche Zartheit und Innigkeit neben
Energie und leidenschaftlicher Kraft, kenntnisreiche Verwendung
der Effekte ohne Effekthascherei, Klarheit und Durchsichtigkeit
neben geistreich verschlungener Arbeit, melodiöse und charakteris-
tische Behandlung des Piano neben so viel Brillianz und Bravour,
dass auch der Virtuose sich dabei befriedigt fühlen kann; kunstle-
rische Einheit in Idee und Ausführung: wo das alles sich vereinigt,
da kann über den Wert einer Komposition wohl kein Zweifel obwal-
ten.' Ibid., 1131, translation mine.

4. 'Wir haben alle Ursache, diese Composition sehr hoch zu stellen und
sie den besten des Tonsetzers anzureihen, namentlich auch deshalb,
weil sie die gewönliche Monotonie der Gattung glücklich vermeidet
und der vollständig obligaten, mit grosser Liebe und Sorgfalt gear-
beiteten Orchesterpartie, ohne den Eindruck der Pianoleistung zu
beeinträchtigen, ihr volles Recht widerfahren läßt und beiden
Theilen ihre Selbständigkeit in schöner Verbindung zu wahren
Weiss. Unter der zahllosen Menge von Ephemeren, welche jede
Woche auf dem Gebiete der Pianofortecomposition erzeugt, thut es
wahrhaft wohl, einmal einem so gediegenen, tüchtigen Werke zu
begegnen ....' See 'Aus Dresden. Concerte', *Allgemeine
Musikalische Zeitung* 1845/52 (31 December 1845): 927–32, at
927–8, translation mine.

5. 'Das neue Pianoforteconcert ihres Gatten ist ein schön empfundenes,
tief durchdachtes und geistreiches Werk, welches einen erfreulichen
Beweis gibt, dass Robert Schumanns ausgezeichnetes Talent mit
seltenem Glücke auch der Composition glänzender Solostücke sich
zuwendet. Damit jedoch der eben gebrauchte Ausdruck nicht zu
Missdeutungen Anlass gebe, fügen wir hinzu: das Concert ist um
deswillen nicht blos in die Reihe der 'Soli' einzurangieren, weil es
nicht wie die Concerte einer gewissen Periode, in Solo- und Tutti-
sätze zerfällt, sondern in symphonischer Weise ein Tongemälde
entwirft, in welchem das Pianoforte die Hauptrolle spielt. Dieser
Wechsel der Farben, dieses Erfassen und gegenseitiger Übertragen
der Selbständigkeit zwischen Orchester und Klavier verleiht dem

Conclusions

Stücke einen besonderen Reiz und bildet es zu einem schönen, abgegrundeten Ganzen.' *Allgemeine musikalische Zeitung* 1846/1 (7 January 1846): 11–13, at 11, translation mine.

6. Eduard Hanslick, *Aus dem Concert-Saal: Kritiken und Schilderungen aus 20 Jahren des Wiener Musiklebens* (Vienna: Wilhelm Braumüller, 1897), 182: 'Dieses Konzert, auf dem Programm als "neu" verzeichnet, ist gleichwohl dasselbe, das wir bereits vor elf Jahren in Wien gehört; Schumann dirigierte es damals, Clara spielte das Klavier. Die Thatsache, daß es seither niemand gespielt hat, kann höchstens in der großen Schwierigkeit desselben Erklärung finden, oder in der noch größeren Indolenz unserer Pianisten.' Translation mine.

7. 'Ein kurze "Allegro molto" schließt den ersten Satz, der somit in seiner Folge von mäßig, rascher, langsamer und schnellster Bewegung selbst das verkleinerte Abbild eines ganzen Concertes ist.' Ibid., translation mine.

8. The first performance of Op. 54 in London I can discover for which Clara Schumann was not the pianist is a Crystal Palace Concert of 4 February 1871, for which the soloist was Oscar Beringer. A report appeared in 'Crystal Palace', *Morning Post* (6 February 1871), British Newspaper Archive.

9. For an overview of Clara's tours, see Reich, *Clara Schumann*, 259–60, and also Ellsworth, 'Women Soloists and the Piano Concerto in Nineteenth-Century London', 44–7. The concert history given here for London is compiled from programmes and reviews available via the British Newspaper Archive, especially as reported in *The Graphic*, the *Daily News*, the *Pall Mall Gazette*, *The Standard* and the *Morning Post*.

10. 'Music: New Philharmonic Society', *Daily News* 3118 (15 March 1856), British Newspaper Archive.

11. 'New Philharmonic Society', *The Standard* 9908 (15 May 1856), British Newspaper Archive.

12. 'Philharmonic Society', *The Standard* 12733 (31 May 1865), British Newspaper Archive.

13. 'Concerts and Music: Philharmonic Society', *The Era* 1392 (4 June 1865), British Newspaper Archive.

14. 'Music: Crystal Palace Concerts', *Daily News* 6793 (10 February 1868), British Newspaper Archive.

15. Unsigned, 'Robert Schumann', *Pall Mall Gazette* 1187 (30 November 1868), British Newspaper Archive.

16. 'Crystal Palace Concerts', *Morning Post* 29705 (22 February 1869), British Newspaper Archive.

17. 'Crystal Palace Concerts', *Morning Post* 29705 (7 March 1870), British Newspaper Archive.

18. 'Concerts, *Pall Mall Gazette* 1580 (7 March 1870), British Newspaper Archive.

19. This list is compiled from a survey of newspaper and periodical sources in the British Newspaper Archive dated from 1 January 1870 to 31 December 1900.

20. www.for3.org/forums/showthread.php?20157-BaL-20-04-19-11-01-20-Schumann-Piano-Concerto-in-A-minor.

21. Hepokoski and Darcy, *Elements of Sonata Theory*, 177–9 and 245–9.

22. Rubinstein's form goes beyond Schumann in other respects. The development begins with the first theme in the tonic before moving off into the development, reflecting a strategy often favoured by Brahms. By way of compensation, the recapitulation begins with the transition and then reprises the second theme in VI. The first theme's absence is compensated by its dramatic tonic return between the end of the cadenza and the coda. Sonata theorists might see this as an expanded type 1 (a binary sonata, in which the space between the return of the first theme and that of the second is expanded by development) or perhaps type 2 (in which the second part of the form is a development fused with the return of the transition and second theme). Given the return of the second theme and closing section in B flat, it is perhaps more reasonable to hear this as a reversed recapitulation with non-tonic second-theme reprise, although this notion is controversial in sonata-theoretical terms. On this, see on the one hand Hepokoski and Darcy, *Elements of Sonata Theory*, 382–3 and James Hepokoski, *A Sonata Theory Handbook* (New York: Oxford University Press, 2021), 198–232, and on the other hand Steven Vande Moortele, *The Romantic Overture and Musical Form from Rossini to Wagner*, 236–40 and 'Apparent Type 2 Sonatas and Reversed Recapitulations in the Nineteenth Century', *Music Analysis* 40/3 (2021): 502–33.

23. The idea that decolonisation should focus on the 'metropole' rather than the former colonies and should therefore turn its attention to the role of classical music in current scholarship is stressed in William Fourie, 'Musicology and Decolonial Analysis in the Age of Brexit', *Twentieth-Century Music* 17/2 (2020): 197–211. On the anti-elitist critique of classical music from a sociological perspective, see Anna Bull, *Class, Control and Classical Music* (New York: Oxford University Press, 2019). The debate about the decolonisation of music curricula entered the British press in the wake of the impact of the 'Rhodes Must Fall' movement on the Oxford Music Faculty, on which see 'Music Notation Branded Colonialist by Oxford Professor Hoping to "Decolonise" the Curriculum', *The Daily Telegraph* (27 March 2021), www.telegraph.co.uk/news/2021/03/27/musical-notations-branded-colonialist-oxford-professors-hoping. For a contextualisation of these

issues in relation to social justice more generally, see Cathy Benedict, Patrick K. Schmidt, Gary Spruce and Paul Woodford, eds., *The Oxford Handbook of Social Justice in Music Education* (New York: Oxford University Press, 2016).

24. I think especially of the argument developed in Richard Taruskin, *The Oxford History of Music. Vol. 1: The Earliest Notation to the Sixteenth Century* (New York: Oxford University Press, 2005), xxiii.

25. Taruskin, *The Oxford History of Music. Vol. 5: The Twentieth Century* (New York: Oxford University Press, 2005), 510.

Glossary of Technical Terms and Symbols

Term	Meaning
A	First theme (in a sonata form), refrain (in a rondo) or first section (in a ternary form).
B	Second theme (in a sonata form), first episode (in a rondo) or contrasting middle section (in a ternary form).
C	Closing section (in a sonata form) or second episode (in a rondo).
TR	Transition: the music that connects a first theme to a second theme (in a sonata form) or a refrain to an episode (in a rondo).
RT	Retransition: the music that connects a development (in a sonata form), B or C section (in a rondo) or B section (in a ternary form) to the reprise of A.
pre-core	The first part of a development section in a sonata form.
core	The central part of a development section in a sonata form.
R	Ritornello (in a type 5 sonata).
S	Solo (in a type 5 sonata).
integer after A, B, etc.	Succession of new material within A, B, etc. (A1, A2, etc.; B1, B2, etc.).
superscript integer after A, B, etc.	Reprise of A, B, etc. (A, A^1, etc.; B, B^1, etc.).
integer after R and S	Succession of ritornelli and solo episodes in a type 5 sonata (for example, R1–S1–R2–S2, etc.).
type I sonata	James Hepokoski and Warren Darcy's term for a sonata without development.

Appendix I

(cont.)

Term	Meaning
type 2 sonata	James Hepokoski and Warren Darcy's term for a binary sonata, in which the second section consists of a development and reprise of the second theme and closing section in the tonic.
type 3 sonata	James Hepokoski and Warren Darcy's term for the standard classical sonata form comprising exposition, development and recapitulation.
type 5 sonata	James Hepokoski and Warren Darcy's term for the combination of sonata form and ritornello form in the first movements of classical concerti.
PAC	Perfect authentic cadence: a cadence in which the bass moves by root motion from dominant to tonic and the soprano reaches the tonic scale-degree above the chord with which the cadence concludes.
IAC	Imperfect authentic cadence: a cadence in which the bass moves by root motion from dominant to tonic and the soprano reaches a scale-degree of the tonic triad other than $\hat{1}$ (that is, $\hat{3}$ or $\hat{5}$) above the chord with which the cadence concludes.
HC	Half-cadence: a cadence concluding with a root-position dominant triad.
DC	Deceptive cadence: a cadence in which the ultimate tonic is displaced by chord vi (in a major key) or chord VI (in a minor key).
EC	Evaded cadence: a cadence in which the final tonic chord is withheld, ordinarily prompting a second attempt at its completion.
EST	Essential sonata trajectory: James Hepokoski and Warren Darcy's term for the important cadential goals that define classical sonata form (abbreviation mine).

Term	Meaning
EEC	Essential expositional closure: the perfect authentic cadence that closes the second theme in a sonata exposition and initiates the closing section.
ESC	Essential structural closure: the perfect authentic cadence that closes the second theme in a sonata recapitulation and initiates the closing section. This is ordinarily a transposition of the EEC into the tonic.
MC	Medial caesura: a cadential or half-cadential pause in the tonic or another key, which completes the transition and heralds the start of a second theme.
two-dimensional sonata form	Steven Vande Moortele's term for a sonata form which also contains sections resembling the movement types of a sonata cycle (first movement, slow movement, *scherzo*, finale).
formal function	William Caplin's term for a unit of music within a single movement that performs one evident formal task at a given formal level.
becoming (functional transformation)	Janet Schmalfeldt's term for the situation in which one formal function retrospectively takes on the role of another.
progressive transformation ($\Rightarrow$)	The situation in which one formal function takes on the role of its expected successor (for example, an introduction 'becomes' a first theme).
regressive transformation ($\Leftarrow$)	The situation in which one formal function takes on the role of its expected predecessor (for example, a first theme 'becomes' an introduction).
circular transformation ($\Leftrightarrow$)	The situation in which two formal functions oscillate (for example, a transition 'becomes' a second theme, which reverts to a transition).

APPENDIX II

Discography

Pianist	Orchestra	Conductor	Label	Year
Géza Anda	SWR Sinfonieorchester des Südwestrundfunks	Ernest Bour	Hänssler Classics	1963
Géza Anda	Berliner Philharmoniker	Raphael Kubelik	Deutsche Grammophon	1967
Leif Ove Andsnes	Berliner Philharmoniker	Mariss Jansons	Warner	2003
Martha Argerich	Washington National Symphony Orchestra	Mstislav Rostropovitch	Deutsche Grammophon	1978
Martha Argerich	Warsaw Philharmonic Orchestra	Kazimierz Kord	FN	1996
Martha Argerich	Orchestra della Svizzera Italiana	Alexandre Rabinovitch-Barakovsky	EMI	2005
Martha Argerich	Gewandhausorchester Leipzig	Riccardo Chailly	Decca	2006
Martha Argerich	Chamber Orchestra of Europe	Nikolaus Harnoncourt	Elatus	2011
Martha Argerich	Orchestra della Svizzera Italiana	Alexander Vedernikov	Deutsche Grammophon	2012
Claudio Arrau	Detroit Symphony Orchestra	Karl Krueger	Victor	1944
Claudio Arrau	New York Philharmonic Orchestra	Victor de Sabata	Aura	2002, live recording
Claudio Arrau	Philharmonia Orchestra	Alceo Galliera	Columbia	1951 1959

Pianist	Orchestra	Conductor	Label	Year
Claudio Arrau	Royal Concertgebouw Orchestra	Christoph von Dohnanyi	Philips	1963
Claudio Arrau	Boston Symphony Orchestra	Sir Colin Davis	Philips	1981
Vladimir Ashkenazy	London Symphony Orchestra	Uri Segal	Decca	1977
Wilhelm Backhaus	Wiener Philharmoniker	Gunter Wand	Decca	1961
Daniel Barenboim	London Philharmonic Orchestra	Dietrich Fischer-Dieskau	HMV	1975
Daniel Barenboim	Münchner Philharmoniker	Sergiu Celibidache	Warner	2002, recorded 1991
Idil Biret	Bilkent Symphony Orchestra	Antoni Wit	Naxos	2000
Felizitas Blumenthal	Vienna Pro Musica Orchestra	Hans Swarowsky	Tuxedo	1990
Alfred Brendel	London Symphony Orchestra	Claudio Abbado	Philips	1980
Alfred Brendel	Wiener Philharmoniker	Sir Simon Rattle	Decca	2018, live recording from 2001
Alfred Brendel	Philharmonia Orchestra	Kurt Sanderling	Philips	2002
Davide Cabassi	Haydn Orchestra of Bolzano and Trento	Gustav Kuhn	Col Legno	2011
Shura Cherkassky	London Philharmonic Orchestra	Sir Adrian Boult	Columbia	1966
Van Cliburn	Chicago Symphony Orchestra	Fritz Reiner	RCA Victor	1960

(cont.)

Pianist	Orchestra	Conductor	Label	Year
Alfred Cortot	London Philharmonic Orchestra	Landon Ronald	Naxos Historical	recorded 1935
Sequeira Costa	Gulbenkian Orchestra	Stephen Gunzenhauser	Marco Polo	1985
Bella Davidovich	Seattle Symphony Orchestra	Gerard Schwarz	CVP	1995
Pavel Egorov	St Petersburg State Academic Capella Orchestra	Cesare Croci	Audiophile	1994
Rudolf Firkusný	Luxembourg Radio Orchestra	Louis de Froment	Turnabout	1972
Annie Fischer	WDR Sinfonieorchester Köln	Joseph Keilberth	ICA	1958
Annie Fischer	SWR Sinfonieorchester Baden-Baden und Freiburg	Hans Rosbaud	SWR	1959
Annie Fischer	Philharmonia Orchestra	Carlo Maria Giulini	Columbia	1963
Annie Fischer	Philharmonia Orchestra	Otto Klemperer	EMI	1963
Leon Fleisher	Cleveland Orchestra	George Szell	Epic	1960
Ingrid Fliter	Scottish Chamber Orchestra	Antonio Mendez	Linn	2016
Samson François	Orchestre National de la Radiodiffusion Française	Paul Kletzki	HMV	1960
Justus Frantz	Wiener Philharmoniker	Leonard Bernstein	Deutsche Grammophon	1985
Nelson Freire	Münchner Philharmoniker	Rudolf Kempe	CBS	1968
Paolo Giacometti	Royal Philharmonic Orchestra of Arnhem	Michel Tilkin	Channel	2002

Performer	Orchestra	Conductor	Label	Date
Walter Gieseking	Staatskapelle Dresden	Karl Böhm	Naxos Historical	recorded 1940–2
Walter Gieseking	Berliner Philharmoniker	Wilhelm Furtwängler	Deutsche Grammophon	1942
Walter Gieseking	Gürzenich-Orchester Köln	Günter Wand	Arkadia	1991, recorded 1951
Walter Gieseking	Philharmonia Orchestra	Herbert von Karajan	Columbia	1954
Emil Gilels	USSR State Symphony Orchestra	Vladimir Verbitsky	Vista Vera	1976
Hélène Grimaud	Deutsches Symphonie-Orchester Berlin	David Zinman	Erato	1995
Hélène Grimaud	Staatskapelle Dresden	Esa-Pekka Salonen	Deutsche Grammophon	2005
Friedrich Gulda	Wiener Symphoniker	Joseph Keilberth	Orfeo	recorded 1955
Friedrich Gulda	Wiener Philharmoniker	Volkmar Andreae	Ace of Clubs	1961
Monique Haas	Berliner Philharmoniker	Eugen Jochum	Deutsche Grammophon	date unknown
Monique Haas	Radio-Sinfonieorchester Stuttgart des SWR	Hans Müller-Kray	SWR	date unknown
Ingrid Haebler	Royal Concertgebouw Orchestra	Eliahu Inbal	Philips	1973
Hubert Harry	Junge Philharmonie Zentralschweiz	Thüring Bräm	Gallo	2010

Pianist	Orchestra	Conductor	Label	Year
Clara Haskil	The Hague Philharmonic Orchestra	Willelm van Otterloo	Philips	1951
Clara Haskil	Danish Radio Orchestra	Rafael Kubelik	Classica Répertoire	2016, recorded 1954
Clara Haskil	Orchestre Philharmonique de Strasbourg	Carl Schuricht	Andromeda	2013, recorded 1955
Clara Haskil	Orchestre de la Suisse Romande	Ernest Ansermet	Claves	recorded 1956
Martin Helmchen	Orchestre Philharmonique de Strasbourg	Marc Albrecht	Pentatone	2009
Dame Myra Hess	Studio Orchestra	Walter Goehr	HMV	1937
Dame Myra Hess	BBC Symphony Orchestra	Sir Malcolm Sargent	BBC	2006, recorded 1958
Dame Myra Hess	Philharmonia Orchestra	Rudolf Schwarz	HMV	date unknown
Angela Hewitt	Deutsches Symphonie-Orchester Berlin	Hannu Lintu	Hyperion	2012
Etsuko Hirose	Orchestre de Pau Pays du Bearn	Fayçal Karoui	Mirare	2011
Margarita Hohenrieder	Neue Philharmonie Westfalen	Johannes Wildner	RCA	2002
Margarita Hohenrieder	Wiener Symphoniker	Fabio Luisi	Solo Musica	2014
Heidrun Holtmann	Berlin Radio Symphony Orchestra	Stefan Soltesz	Laserlight	1994

Pianist	Orchestra	Conductor	Label	Year
Stephen Hough	City of Birmingham Symphony Orchestra	Andris Nelsons	Hyperion	2016
Eugene Istomin	Columbia Symphony Orchestra	Bruno Walter	Philips	1962
Jeno Jandó	Budapest Symphony Orchestra	Andras Ligeti	Naxos	1988
Byron Janis	Chicago Symphony Orchestra	Fritz Reiner	RCA	1983, recorded 1959
Byron Janis	Minneapolis Symphony Orchestra	Stanislaw Skrowaczewski	Mercury	1964
Julian Von Karolyi	Symphonie-Orchester des Bayerischen Rundfunks	Robert Heger	Doremi	2013, recorded 1956
Julius Katchen	Israel Philharmonic Orchestra	Istvan Kertesz	Ace of Diamonds	1974
Peter Katin	London Symphony Orchestra	Sir Eugene Goossens	Everest	1960
Cyprien Katsaris	Japan Philharmonic Orchestra	Cristian Mandeal	Piano 21	2010
Wilhelm Kempff	Orchestre de la Suisse Romande	Ernest Ansermet	Deutsche Grammophon	1959
Wilhelm Kempff	Symphonie-Orchester des Bayerischen Rundfunks	Rafael Kubelik	Deutsche Grammophon	1974
Matthias Kirschnereit	Konzerthaus Orchester Berlin	Jan Willem de Vriend	Berlin	2019
Evgeny Kissin	Vienna Philharmonic Orchestra	Carlo Maria Giulini	Sony	1993

Pianist	Orchestra	Conductor	Label	Year
Evgeny Kissin	London Symphony Orchestra	Sir Colin Davis	EMI	2007
Anton Kuerti	CBC Radio Orchestra	Mario Bernardi	CBC	2002
Alicia de Larrocha	London Symphony Orchestra	Sir Colin Davis	RCA	1993
Alicia de Larrocha	Royal Philharmonic Orchestra	Charles Dutoit	Decca	1981
Daniel Levy	Philharmonia Orchestra	Dietrich Fischer-Dieskau	Edelweiss	recorded 1998
Dinu Lipatti	Orchestre de la Suisse Romande	Ernest Ansermet	Decca	1970, recorded 1950
Dinu Lipatti	Philharmonia Orchestra	Herbert von Karajan	EMI	1954
Jan Lisiecki	Orchestra dell'Accademia Nazionale di Santa Cecilia	Antonio Pappano	Deutsche Grammophon	2016
Alexander Lonquich	Colibri Ensemble	-	Odradek	2018
Louis Lortie	Philharmonia Orchestra	Neeme Järvi	Chandos	2010
Jean-Marc Luisada	London Symphony Orchestra	Michael Tilson Thomas	Deutsche Grammophon	1994
Benedetto Lupo	Orchestra della Svizzera Italiana	Peter Maag	Arts	1999
Radu Lupu	London Symphony Orchestra	André Previn	Decca	1973
Moura Lympany	Royal Philharmonic Orchestra	Sir Thomas Beecham	Somm	2006, recorded 1946

Israela Margalit	London Philharmonic Orchestra	Bryden Thomson	Chandos	1987
Oleg Marshev	South Jutland Symphony Orchestra	Vladimir Ziva	Danacord	2011
Alexander Meinel	Erzgebirgische Philharmonie Aue	Naoshi Takahashi	Querstand	2013
Alexander Melnikov	Freiburger Barockorchester	Pablo Heras-Casado	Harmonia Mundi	2015
Janne Mertanen	Gävle Symphony Orchestra	Hannu Koivula	Alba	2013
Arturo Benedetti Michelangeli	New York Philharmonic	Dimitri Mitropoulos	Fabula	2011, live recording 1948
Arturo Benedetti Michelangeli	RTSI Orchestra	Hermann Scherchen	Concordia	1986, live recording 1956
Arturo Benedetti Michelangeli	Orchestra Sinfonica di Roma della RAI	Gianandrea Gavazzeni	Warner	2001, recorded 1962
Arturo Benedetti Michelangeli	Orchestre de Paris	Daniel Barenboim	Deutsche Grammophon	2009, recorded 1984
Tee Min	Orchestra 'New Philharmony' St Petersburg	Alexander Titov	Digital Focus	1993
Ivan Moravec	Czech Philharmonic Orchestra	Vaclav Neumann	Supraphon	1977

Pianist	Orchestra	Conductor	Label	Year
Ivan Moravec	Dallas Symphony Orchestra	Eduardo Mata	Dorian	1993
Branka Musulin	Radio-Sinfonieorchester Stuttgart des SWR	Karl Böhm	SWR	2018, recorded 1954
Yves Nat	Lamoureux Orchestra	Eugene Bigot	Columbia	1949
Yves Nat	Orchestre National de la Radiodiffusion Française	Charles Munch	HMV	1980, recorded 1957
Guiomar Novaes	Wiener Symphoniker	Otto Klemperer	Vox	1972
Gerhard Oppitz	Bamberger Symphoniker	Marc Andrae	Tudor	2012
Gerhard Oppitz	NDR Sinfonieorchester	Günter Wand	Profil	2013, date of recording unknown
Cécile Ousset	London Philharmonic Orchestra	Kurt Masur	Warner	1999
Sophie Pacini	Deutsche Staatsphilharmonie Rheinland-Pfalz	Radoslaw Szulc	Onyx	2012
Lucy Parham	BBC Concert Orchestra	Barry Wordsworth	Sanctuary	2004
Leonard Pennario	London Symphony Orchestra	Seiji Ozawa	RCA	1966
Murray Perahia	Bavarian Radio Symphony Orchestra	Sir Colin Davis	CBS	1989
Murray Perahia	Berliner Philharmoniker	Claudio Abbado	Sony	1997
Francesco Piemontesi	BBC Symphony Orchestra	Jiri Belohlávek	Naïve	2012

Maria João Pires	Chamber Orchestra of Europe	Claudio Abbado	Deutsche Grammophon	2000
Maria João Pires	London Symphony Orchestra	Sir John Eliot Gardiner	LSO Live	2014
Maurizio Pollini	Berliner Philharmoniker	Claudio Abbado	Deutsche Grammophon	1990
Sviatoslav Richter	USSR State Orchestra	George Georgescu	Legendary Treasures	2007, recorded 1958
Sviatoslav Richter	Moscow Radio Orchestra	Alexander Gauk	Monitor	1960
Sviatoslav Richter	Vienna Philharmonic Orchestra	Riccardo Muti	Orfeo	1998, recorded 1972
Sviatoslav Richter	USSR State Symphony Orchestra	Rudolf Barshai	Melodiya	1973
Sviatoslav Richter	L'Orchestre National de l'Opéra de Monte-Carlo	Lovro von Matacic	EMI	1975
Sviatoslav Richter	Hungarian State Philharmonic Orchestra	János Ferencsik	Hungaroton	1978
Sviatoslav Richter	Warsaw National Philharmonic Orchestra	Stanislav Wislocki	Deutsche Grammophon	1983
Bruno Rigutto	Orchestre National de France	Kurt Masur	IPG	1977
Gerald Robbins	Moscow Philharmonic Orchestra	Kenneth Klein	MSR	2009
Peter Rösel	Gewandhausorchester Leipzig	Kurt Masur	Eterna	1980

(cont.)

Pianist	Orchestra	Conductor	Label	Year
Arthur Rubinstein	RCA Victor Symphony Orchestra	William Steinberg	RCA	1950
Arthur Rubinstein	RCA Victor Symphony Orchestra	Josef Krips	RCA	1959
Arthur Rubinstein	Orchestra Alessandro Scarlatti di Napoli della RAI	Franco Caracciolo	Arts	2009, recorded 1964
Arthur Rubinstein	Chicago Symphony Orchestra	Carlo Maria Giulini	RCA	1968
Emil von Sauer	Royal Concertgebouw Orchestra	Willem Mengelberg	Melodiya	1983, recorded 1940
Sir András Schiff	Royal Concertgebouw Orchestra	Antal Dorati	London	1985
Artur Schnabel	Philharmonic-Symphony Orchestra	Pierre Monteux	Music and Arts	recorded 1943
Rudolf Serkin	Philadelphia Orchestra	Eugene Ormandy	Columbia	1964
Regina Shamvili	Ecuador National Symphony Orchestra	Alvaro Manzano	VDE-Gallo	2010
Howard Shelley	Orchestra of Opera North	-	Chandos	2008
Solomon	Philharmonia Orchestra	Herbert Menges	HMV	1955
Martin Stadtfeld	Hallé Orchestra	Sir Mark Elder	Sony	2015

Performer	Orchestra	Conductor	Label	Year
Andreas Staier	Orchestre des Champs-Élysées	Philippe Herreweghe	Harmonia Mundi	1996
Richard Tilling	Plovdiv Philharmonic Orchestra	-	Resonance	2007
Dubravka Tomsic	Slovenian Symphony Orchestra	Anton Nanut	Grand Gala	1991
Dénes Várjon	WDR Sinfonieorchester Köln	Heinz Holliger	Audite	2016
Lev Vinocour	ORF Vienna Radio Symphony Orchestra	Johannes Wildner	RCA	2013
Lars Vogt	City of Birmingham Symphony Orchestra	Sir Simon Rattle	EMI	1992
Shai Wosner	Chamber Orchestra of Philadelphia	Lawrence Foster	Chamber Orchestra of Philadelphia	2014
Klára Würtz	North-West German Philharmonic Orchestra	Arie van Beek	Brilliant	2001
Christian Zacharias	Orchestre de Chambre de Lausanne	-	MDG	2002
Christian Zacharias	WDR Sinfonieorchester Köln	Hans Vonk	Warner	2008
Krystian Zimerman	Berliner Philharmoniker	Herbert von Karajan	Deutsche Grammophon	1982

BIBLIOGRAPHY

Amster, Isabella, *Das Virtuosenkonzert in der ersten Hälfte des 19. Jahrhunderts* (Wolfenbüttel: Kallmeyer, 1931).

Anon., 'Music: New Philharmonic Society', *Daily News* 3118 (15 March 1856), British Newspaper Archive.

Anon., 'New Philharmonic Society', *The Standard* 9908 (15 May 1856), British Newspaper Archive.

Anon., 'Philharmonic Society', *The Standard* 12733 (31 May 1865), British Newspaper Archive.

Anon., 'Concerts and Music: Philharmonic Society', *The Era* 1392 (4 June 1865), British Newspaper Archive.

Anon., 'Music: Crystal Palace Concerts', *Daily News* 6793 (10 February 1868), British Newspaper Archive.

Anon., 'Robert Schumann', *Pall Mall Gazette* 1187 (30 November 1868), British Newspaper Archive.

Anon., 'Crystal Palace Concerts', *Morning Post* 29705 (22 February 1869), British Newspaper Archive.

Anon., 'Concerts', *Pall Mall Gazette* 1580 (7 March 1870), British Newspaper Archive.

Anon., 'Crystal Palace Concerts', *Morning Post* 29705 (7 March 1870), British Newspaper Archive.

Anon., 'Crystal Palace', *Morning Post* (6 February 1871), British Newspaper Archive.

Appel, Bernhard, 'Die Überleitung vom 2. zum 3. Satz in Robert Schumanns Klavierkonzert Opus 54', *Musikforschung* 44 (1991): 255–61.

Appel, Bernhard, 'Kulturgut oder Kapitalanlage? Zum Ankauf des Autographs von Robert Schumanns Klavierkonzert Op. 54', *Neue Zeitschrift für Musik* 151 (1990): 11–12.

Applegate, Celia, *The Necessity of Music: Variations on a German Theme* (Toronto: University of Toronto Press, 2017).

Applegate, Celia, 'Robert Schumann and the Culture of German Nationhood', in Roe-Min Kok and Laura Tunbridge, eds., *Rethinking Schumann* (New York: Oxford University Press, 2011), 3–14.

Becker, Carl Friedrich, 'Pianoforte: Concerte', *Neue Zeitschrift für Musik* 6/14 (1837): 56–7.

Benedict, Cathy, Patrick K. Schmidt, Gary Spruce and Paul Woodford, eds., *The Oxford Handbook of Social Justice in Music Education* (New York: Oxford University Press, 2016).

194

Bibliography

Boetticher, Wolfgang, 'Das Entstehen von R. Schumanns Klavierkonzert: Textkritische Studien', in *Festschrift Martin Ruhnke zum 65. Geburtstag* (Stuttgart: Hänssler-Verlag, 1986), 45–55.

Boetticher, Wolfgang, 'Preface', in Robert Schumann, *Phantasie for Piano and Orchestra in A Minor*, WoO, ed. Wolfgang Boetticher (London: Ernst Eulenburg, 1994), iii–xix.

Boland, Majella, 'John Field in Context: A Reappraisal of the Nocturnes and Piano Concerti' (PhD dissertation: University College Dublin, 2013).

Bonds, Mark Evan, *Music As Thought: Listening to the Symphony in the Age of Beethoven* (Princeton, NJ: Princeton University Press, 2006).

Bull, Anna, *Class, Control and Classical Music* (New York: Oxford University Press, 2019).

Caplin, William E., *Analyzing Classical Form: An Approach for the Classroom* (New York: Oxford University Press, 2013).

Caplin, William E., 'Beyond the Classical Cadence: Thematic Closure in Early Romantic Music', *Music Theory Spectrum* 40/1 (2018): 1–26.

Caplin, William E., 'The Classical Cadence: Conceptions and Misconceptions', *Journal of the American Musicological Society* 57/1 (2004): 51–118.

Caplin, William E., 'What Are Formal Functions?', in Pieter Bergé, ed., *Musical Form, Forms and Formenlehre: Three Methodological Reflections* (Leuven: Leuven University Press, 2010), 21–40.

Carew, Derek, *The Mechanical Muse: The Piano, Pianism and Piano Music, c. 1760–1850* (Aldershot: Ashgate, 2007).

Carner, Mosco, 'The Orchestral Music', in Gerald Abraham, ed., *Schumann: A Symposium* (London: Oxford University Press, 1952), 176–244.

Chissell, Joan, *Clara Schumann: A Dedicated Spirit* (London: Hamish Hamilton, 1983).

Cohn, Richard, 'Maximally Smooth Cycles, Hexatonic Systems and the Analysis of Late-Romantic Triadic Progressions', *Music Analysis* 15/1 (1996): 9–40.

Dahlhaus, Carl, *Nineteenth-Century Music*, trans. J. Bradford Robinson (Berkeley: University of California Press, 1989).

Daverio, John, *Robert Schumann: Herald of a New Poetic Age* (Oxford: Oxford University Press, 1997).

Daverio, John, 'Schumann's System of Musical Fragments and *Witz*', in *Nineteenth-Century Music and the German Romantic Ideology* (New York: Schirmer, 1993), 49–88.

Davies, Joe, 'Clara Schumann and the Nineteenth-Century Piano Concerto', in Joe Davies, ed., *Clara Schumann Studies* (Cambridge: Cambridge University Press, 2021), 95–116.

Dörffel, Alfred, *Statistik der Concerte im Saale des Gewandhauses zu Leipzig, 25 November 1781–25 November 1881* (Leipzig: Breitkopf und Härtel, 1881).

Draheim, Joachim, 'Preface', in Robert Schumann, *Konzertsatz für Klavier und Orchester D-Moll*, reconstructed and completed by Jozef De Beenhouwer, ed. Joachim Draheim (Wiesbaden: Breitkopf und Härtel, 1988), i–xii.

Bibliography

Eismann, Georg, *Robert Schumann: Ein Quellenwerk über sein Leben und Schaffen*, vol. I (Leipzig: Breitkopf und Härtel, 1956).

Ellsworth, Therese, 'Women Soloists and the Piano Concerto in Nineteenth-Century London', in Therese Ellsworth and Susan Wollenberg, eds., *The Piano in Nineteenth-Century British Culture: Instruments, Performers and Repertoire* (Aldershot: Ashgate, 2007), 21–49.

Fourie, William, 'Musicology and Decolonial Analysis in the Age of Brexit', *Twentieth-Century Music* 17/2 (2020): 197–211.

Fox, Margaret Elizabeth, 'Deciphering the Arabesque: Genre Mixture and Formal Digression in the Early Romantic Piano Concerto' (PhD dissertation: University of Toronto, 2021).

Fuhrmann, Wolfgang, 'The Intimate Art of Listening: Music in the Private Sphere during the Nineteenth Century', in Christian Thorau and Hansjakob Ziemer, eds., *The Oxford Handbook of Music Listening in the Nineteenth and Twentieth Centuries* (New York: Oxford University Press, 2019), 284–311.

Garratt, James, *Music, Culture and Social Reform in the Age of Wagner* (Cambridge: Cambridge University Press, 2010).

Gauldin, Robert, 'New Twists for Old Endings: Cadenza and Apotheosis in the Romantic Piano Concerto', *Intégral* 18–19 (2004–5): 1–23.

Gerstmeier, August, *Robert Schumann: Klavierkonzert A-moll, Op. 54* (Munich: Wilhelm Fink Verlag, 1986).

Gooley, Dana, 'The Battle against Instrumental Virtuosity in the Early Nineteenth Century', in Christopher H. Gibbs and Dana Gooley, eds., *Franz Liszt and His World* (Princeton, NJ: Princeton University Press, 2006), 75–111.

Habermas, Jürgen, *The Structural Transformation of the Public Sphere: An Enquiry into a Category of Bourgeois Society* (Cambridge: Polity Press, 1989).

Hagels, Bert, *Konzerte in Leipzig, 1779/80–1847/48* (Berlin: Ries & Erler, 2009).

Hamilton, Kenneth, *After the Golden Age* (New York: Oxford University Press, 2007).

Hepokoski, James, *A Sonata Theory Handbook* (New York: Oxford University Press, 2021).

Hepokoski, James, 'Monumentality and Formal Process in the First Movement of Brahms's Piano Concerto No. 1 in D Minor, Op. 15', in Heather Platt and Peter H. Smith, eds., *Expressive Intersections in Brahms: Essays in Analysis and Meaning* (Bloomington: Indiana University Press, 2012), 217–51.

Hepokoski, James and Warren Darcy, *Elements of Sonata Theory: Norms, Types, and Deformations in the Late-Eighteenth-Century Sonata* (New York: Oxford University Press, 2006).

Horton, Julian, 'Beethoven's Error? The Modulating Ritornello and the Type-5 Sonata in the Post-Classical Piano Concerto', *Music Analysis* 40/3 (2021): 353–412.

Horton, Julian, *Brahms's Piano Concerto No. 2, Op. 83: Analytical and Contextual Studies* (Leuven: Peeters, 2017).

Bibliography

Horton, Julian, 'Formal Type and Formal Function in the Post-Classical Piano Concerto', in Julie Pedneault-Deslauriers, Nathan John Martin and Steven Vande Moortele, eds., *Formal Functions in Perspective: Essays in Musical Form from Haydn to Adorno* (Rochester, NY: University of Rochester Press, 2015), 77–122.

Horton, Julian, 'John Field and the Alternative History of Concerto First-Movement Form', *Music & Letters* 92/1 (2011): 43–83.

Horton, Julian, 'Rethinking Sonata Failure: Mendelssohn's Overture *Zum Märchen von der schönen Melusine*', *Music Theory Spectrum* 43/2 (2021): 299–319.

Ivanovich, Roman, 'The Brilliant Style', in Danuta Mirka, ed., *The Oxford Handbook of Topic Theory* (New York: Oxford University Press, 2014), 330–54.

Kang, Man-Hee, 'Robert Schumann's Piano Concerto in A Minor, Op. 54: A Stemmatic Analysis of the Sources' (PhD dissertation: Ohio State University, 1992).

Keefe, Simon P., 'Dramatic Dialogue in Mozart's Viennese Piano Concertos: A Study of Competition and Cooperation in Three First Movements', *Musical Quarterly* 83/2 (1999): 169–204.

Keefe, Simon P., *Mozart's Piano Concertos: Dramatic Dialogue in the Age of Enlightenment* (Woodbridge: Boydell, 2001).

Kerman, Joseph, 'The Concertos', in Beate Perrey, ed., *The Cambridge Companion to Schumann* (Cambridge: Cambridge University Press, 2007), 173–94.

Klassen, Janina, '"Schumann will es nun instrumentieren": Das Finale aus Clara Wiecks Klavierkonzert Op. 7 als frühestes Beispiel einer künstlerischen Zusammenarbeit von Robert und Clara Schumann', *Schumann-Studien* 3/4 (1994): 291–9.

Koch, Juan Martin, *Das Klavierkonzert des 19. Jahrhunderts und die Kategorie des Symphonischen* (Sinzing: Studio, 2001).

Krebs, Harald, *Fantasy Pieces: Metrical Dissonance in the Music of Robert Schumann* (Oxford: Oxford University Press, 1999).

L. R., 'Elftes Abonnement-Concert', *Allgemeine musikalische Zeitung* 1846/1 (7 January 1846): 11–13.

Lindeman, Stephan D., *Structural Novelty and Tradition in the Early Romantic Piano Concerto* (Stuyvesant: Pendragon Press, 1999).

Liszt, Franz, 'Prämium-Beigabe zu John Field, Nocturnes', trans. Julius Schuberth, in Franz Liszt, ed., *John Field: 18 Nocturnes* (J. Schuberth: Leipzig, 1859), 1–8.

Macdonald, Claudia, 'Critical Perception and the Woman Composer: The Early Reception of Piano Concertos by Clara Wieck Schumann and Amy Beach', *Current Musicology* 55 (1993): 24–55.

Macdonald, Claudia, 'Mit einer eignen außerordentlichen Composition: The Genesis of Schumann's *Phantasie* in A Minor', *Journal of Musicology* 13/2 (1995): 240–59.

Bibliography

Macdonald, Claudia, *Robert Schumann and the Piano Concerto* (New York: Routledge, 2005).

Macdonald, Claudia, 'Robert Schumann's F Major Concerto of 1831 As Reconstructed from His First Sketchbook: A History of Its Composition and Study of Its Musical Background' (PhD dissertation: University of Chicago, 1986).

Mak, Su-Yin, 'Schubert's Sonata Forms and the Poetics of the Lyric', *Journal of Musicology* 23/2 (2006): 263–306.

Martin, Nathan John, 'Schumann's Fragment', *Indiana Theory Review* 28/1–2 (2010): 85–109.

Martin, Nathan John and Steven Vande Moortele, 'Formal Functions and Retrospective Reinterpretation in the First Movement of Schubert's String Quintet', *Music Analysis* 33/2 (2014): 130–55.

Mirka, Danuta, 'Introduction', in Danuta Mirka, ed., *The Oxford Handbook of Topic Theory* (Oxford: Oxford University Press, 2014), 1–60.

Parham, Lucy, 'Schumann, Piano Concerto in A Minor, Op. 54', Building a Library, the New Radio 3 Forum: www.for3.org/forums/showthread.php?20157-BaL-20-04-19-11-01-20-Schumann-Piano-Concerto-in-A-minor.

Plantinga, Leon, *Schumann as Critic* (New Haven, CT: Yale University Press, 1967).

Ratner, Leonard, *Classic Music: Expression, Form and Style* (New York: Schirmer, 1980), 19.

Reich, Nancy, *Clara Schumann: The Artist and the Woman* (Ithaca, NY: Cornell University Press, 2013).

Retallack, James, ed., *Saxony in German History: Culture, Society, and Politics, 1830–1933* (Ann Arbor: University of Michigan Press, 2000).

Rink, John, *Chopin: The Piano Concertos* (Cambridge: Cambridge University Press, 1997).

Roe, Stephen, 'The Autograph Manuscript of Schumann's Piano Concerto', *Musical Times* 131/1764 (1990): 77–9.

Roeder, Michael Thomas, *A History of the Concerto* (Portland, OR: Amadeus Press, 1994).

Rowland, David, *A History of Pianoforte Pedalling* (Cambridge: Cambridge University Press, 1993).

Samson, Jim, *The Music of Chopin* (Oxford: Clarendon Press, 1994).

Samson, Jim, *Virtuosity and the Musical Work: The Transcendental Studies of Liszt* (Cambridge: Cambridge University Press, 2003).

Schladebach, Julius ('Wise'), 'Aus Dresden. Concerte', *Allgemeine Musikalische Zeitung* 1845/52 (31 December 1845): 927–32.

Schlegel, Friedrich, *Philosophical Fragments*, trans. Peter Firchow (Minneapolis: University of Minnesota Press, 1991).

Schmalfeldt, Janet, 'Cadential Processes: The Evaded Cadence and the "One-More-Time" Technique', *Journal of Musicological Research* 12 (1992): 1–52.

Schmalfeldt, Janet, *In the Process of Becoming: Analytic and Philosophical Perspectives on Form in Early Nineteenth-Century Music* (New York: Oxford University Press, 2011).

Bibliography

Schoenberg, Arnold, *Fundamentals of Musical Composition*, ed. Gerald Strang (London: Faber and Faber, 1967).

Schubring, Adolph, 'Schumanniana No. 4: The Present Musical Epoch and Robert Schumann's Position in Music History (1861)', trans. John Michael Cooper, in R. Larry Todd, ed., *Schumann and His World* (Princeton, NJ: Princeton University Press), 362–74.

Schumann, Clara and Robert Schuman, *Briefwechsel: Kritische Gesamtausgabe*, 2 vols., ed. Eva Weissweiler (Frankfurt: Stroemfeld/Roter Stern, 1984).

Schumann, Robert, 'Das Clavier-Concert', *Neue Zeitschrift für Musik* 10/2 (1839): 5–7.

Schumann, Robert, 'Fragmente aus Leipzig 4', *Neue Zeitschrift für Musik* 7/19 (1837): 73–5.

Schumann, Robert, 'Pianoforte: Concerte', *Neue Zeitschrift für Musik* 4/18 (1836): 77.

Schumann, Robert, 'Pianoforte: Concerte', *Neue Zeitschrift für Musik* 4/26 (1836): 110–11.

Schumann, Robert, 'Pianoforte: Concerte', *Neue Zeitschrift für Musik* 4/27 (1836): 113–16.

Schumann, Robert, 'Pianoforte: Concerte', *Neue Zeitschrift für Musik* 4/29 (1836): 122–4.

Schumann, Robert, *Tagebücher, Vol. 1: 1827–1838*, ed. Georg Eismann (Leipzig: Deutscher Verlag für Musik, 1971).

Schumann, Robert, *Tagebücher, Vol. 2: 1836–1854*, ed. Gerd Nauhaus (Leipzig: VEB Deutscher Verlag für Musik, 1987).

Schumann, Robert, *Tagebücher, Vol. 3: 1837–1847*, ed. Gerd Nauhaus (Leipzig: VEB Deutscher Verlag für Musik, 1982).

Schumann, Robert, 'Über Genial- Knill- Original- und andre -Itäten', in Frauke Otto, ed., *Schumann als Jean Paul-Leser* (Frankfurt: Herchen Verlag, 1984), 111–13.

'Serpentin', 'Schwärmbriefe: an Chiara', *Neue Zeitschrift für Musik* 3/46 (1835): 182–3.

Simpson, Craig, 'Music Notation Branded Colonialist by Oxford Professor Hoping to "Decolonise" the Curriculum', *The Daily Telegraph* (27 March 2021).

Smith, Peter H., 'Dvořák's Violin Concerto Reconsidered: Joachim's Influence, Bruch's Model and Romantic Innovations in Sonata Practice', *Music Analysis* 41/1 (2022): 3–49.

Taruskin, Richard, *The Oxford History of Music, Vol. 1: The Earliest Notation to the Sixteenth Century* (New York: Oxford University Press, 2005).

Taruskin, Richard, *The Oxford History of Music, Vol. 5: The Twentieth Century* (New York: Oxford University Press, 2005).

Taylor, Benedict, 'Clara Wieck's A Minor Piano Concerto: Formal Innovation and the Problem of Parametric Disconnect in Early Romantic Music', *Music Theory and Analysis* 8/11 (2021): 1–28.

Bibliography

Taylor, Benedict, 'Mutual Deformity: Moscheles's Seventh and Bennett's Fourth Concertos', *Music Analysis* 35/1 (2016): 75–109.

Temperley, Nicholas, 'John Field and the First Nocturne', *Music & Letters* 56/3–4 (1975): 335–40.

Tovey, Donald Francis, 'C: Beethoven, Pianoforte Concerto in C Major, Op. 15', in *Essays in Musical Analysis, Vol. 3: Concertos* (London: Oxford University Press, 1936), 64–9.

Tovey, Donald Francis, 'CXX: Mendelssohn, Violin Concerto in E Minor, Op. 64', in *Essays in Musical Analysis, Vol. 3: Concertos*, 178–81.

Tovey, Donald Francis, 'CXXI: Schumann, Pianoforte Concerto in A Minor, Op. 54', in *Essays in Musical Analysis, Vol. 3: Concertos*, 182–4.

Tovey, Donald Francis, 'LXXXV: The Classical Concerto', in *Essays in Musical Analysis, Vol. 3: Concertos*, 3–27.

Vande Moortele, Steven, *The Romantic Overture and Musical Form from Rossini to Wagner* (Cambridge: Cambridge University Press, 2017).

Vande Moortele, Steven, *Two-Dimensional Sonata Form: Form and Cycle in Single-Movement Instrumental Works by Liszt, Strauss, Schoenberg, and Zemlinsky* (Leuven: Leuven University Press, 2009).

Vosteen, Annette, 'Introduction: *Neue Zeitschrift für Musik* (1834–44)', *Repertoire internationale de la presse musicale* (2001), www.ripm.org/pdf/Introductions/NZM1834-1844introEnglish.pdf.

W. J. S. E., 'Concert. Monat December', *Dresdner Abendzeitung* 103 (25 December 1845): 1130–2.

Weingartner, Felix, 'Schumann as Symphonist (1904–1906)', in R. Larry Todd, ed., *Schumann and His World* (Princeton, NJ: Princeton University Press, 1994), 375–84.

INDEX

Index

Index

Index

Printed in the United States
by Baker & Taylor Publisher Services